£1.49

Iron H of t Dragon's Touch

Secrets of Breaking Power

Iron Hand
of the
Dragon's
Touch
Secrets of
Breaking Power

MASTER HEI LONG

CITADEL PRESS
Kensington Publishing Corp.
www.kensingtonbooks.com

Also by Master Hei Long:

Advanced Dragon's Touch
Da Zhimingde: Striking Deadly Blows to Vital Organs
Dragons Touch: Weaknesses of the Human Anatomy
Gouzao Gongji: Seven Neurological Attacks for Inflicting Serious Damage
Guge Gongji: Seven Primary Targets to Take Anyone Out of a Fight
Master's Guide to Basic Self-Defense: Progressive Retraining of the
   Reflexive Response

CITADEL PRESS BOOKS are published by

Kensington Publishing Corp.
850 Third Avenue
New York, NY 10022

Previously published by Paladin Press

All Kensington titles, imprints, and distributed lines are available at special
quantity discounts for bulk purchases for sales promotions, premiums,
fund-raising, educational, or institutional use. Special book excerpts or
customized printings can also be created to fit specific needs. For details,
write or phone the office of the Kensington special sales manager:
Kensington Publishing Corp., 850 Third Avenue, New York, NY 10022,
attn: Special Sales Department, phone 1-800-221-2647.

First printing: May 2005

10   9   8   7   6   5   4   3   2   1

Printed in the United States of America

Cataloging data may be obtained from the Library of Congress.

ISBN 0-8065-2688-2

Contents

Introduction

Breaking skills may very well be the most coveted aspect of the martial arts, perhaps even beyond the applied technical abilities for self-defense. In demonstrations, observers will be more impressed by breaking than by a smooth, effective technique, even if the break is a relatively simple one. There is a mystique surrounding breaking skills that, like any other science, can be broken down to a simple formula once the stage presence is removed. This is not to take away from the complexities involved, because they are certainly there, but a methodical, knowledgeable approach to gaining the proper skill can and will put that same awesome power into your hands and feet. Once there is a method established and adhered to, it is just a matter of time and patience. To be an accomplished expert in breaking also requires the one element that few people have. It is the final ingredient that determines whether an individual will be a mere practitioner or a champion in his endeavor. It is the one ingredient that is a common factor to every champion in every competitive field: an unyielding determination. Without determination, you will not make it past the first ninety days of training. Although the method is here before you, it will be meaningless if you are not determined to accomplish the task and achieve the skill. Set your goals before you start, and decide now that you are going to spend the time training regardless of how many catastrophes come into your life. Separate your life totally from the time and days you set up for training. The conditioning process will get discouraging at times, and at other times it may even get boring. Keep your mind on the light at the end of the tunnel; it is the long-term accomplishment you are seeking, and it is there waiting for a champion to claim it.

Chapter 1

The Physics of Breaking

Regardless of the art you study, be it a martial art, gymnastics, or even sculpting, the greater the foundation of knowledge you have in the subject, the more likely you are to succeed in mastering that art. Although it is only one of many facets of the martial arts, breaking requires no less of a basic understanding. There is much more involved here than simply callousing your hands and feet and building up enough power to overcome a chosen target. There are thousands of good black belts in this country who quickly ended their careers in breaking because they accelerated their training beyond what their bodies were able to adjust to in the time spent, and there are just as many who damaged their hands and feet simply because of the lack of knowledge of the anatomy of the weapons they were developing. The anatomy of each weapon you will be training is discussed in Chapters Two and Three. In this chapter we are going to try to reach an understanding of the physics of breaking based on the teachings of two men out of history, the physicist Sir Isaac Newton, and the Greek philosopher Pyrrho. A look at their teachings should give you an understanding of how your body is going to react to your breaking efforts, and from this understanding will come wisdom in the art of breaking which in all probability will determine whether you succeed or fail.

Pyrrho lived from 365 BC. to 295 BC. His was the first philosophy centered in skepticism. His teaching was essentially this: all terms of judgment are relative. Unless a defined starting point for reasoning can be established, no criterion of judgment can be valid. What is heavy to one man will be light to another, and in the study at hand, what is hard to one man may be soft to another. Our first learning from Pyrrho's teaching is that where you start in terms of target density or how hard you are able to hit a practice block is going to be determined by your individual body structure and strength. You may build a training block and work on it for six months and still not be able to hit it full power, whereas someone else who has never trained in breaking before may be able to hit that same training block full power with no pain or injury. This does not mean you are training improperly, nor does it mean that you should start hitting the block as hard as you can regardless of how much it hurts. Allow your body to develop at its own pace. If you overload an electrical circuit, it is going to burn up or shut down at a safety switch. Your body is going to do the same thing, but it will speak to you in terms of pain and structural damage. Once you have injured an area of the hand or foot in training, it could be as long as a month or even a year until you can resume training again. How fast you develop your weapons is of no significance. Your body can only recover as fast as its natural ability allows it to recover and be ready for the next training session. True, you must be prepared to endure some physical discomfort and pain, and only you can determine where the stopping point is, but set your standards by your knowledge and experience, not by what another practitioner is capable of doing. As long as you are making progress, care not for your immediate abilities. Steady progress will ensure success in the long run.

Again, Pyrrho's skepticism is a noteworthy teaching in terms of relativity. When I completed *Dragons Touch*, I wanted to add a chapter to it that would give an approximate weight force to apply to anatomical targets to cause a certain bone to break, for example, or to traumatize a nerve complex. I wanted this same impact force in pounds per square inch in numerical figures for one-inch boards. What I was trying to establish was a basic formula that would allow a student to be able to determine whether he had the ability to snap a knee joint with a crossing side kick by being able to break a certain number of boards with the same kick. I intended to take an average man, determine the strength of each area of the body and give an approximate weight force to apply to each pressure point, and give a parallel in boards. Had this been possible, a certain number of boards being broken with a certain type of kick or blow would tell the student he was capable of damaging that specific area, and allow the student to practice and develop the strikes accordingly. A rather long study ended in a conversation with a professor at the University of Florida where I was told that water content determines the strength of boards, and other variables that are too numerous to mention here determine the strength of bones and other areas of the body. Even in ten men of the same height and weight, the variables were too great to give a safe average. As for the strength of wood, a single five-foot section of a two-by-four was cut into five one-foot sections and tested for strength in an experiment. Each section, although it had been cut from the same five-foot piece, varied in strength as much as 35 percent. Pyrrho could not accept a judgment unless he could first establish a defined starting point. This same principle applies in your training. Your starting point is relative, and your rate of progress will be relative. Because water content determines the strength of boards and bricks and other variables determine the strength of the body structure, a careful self-study and awareness will be necessary to train progressively without injury. Never use chemicals or drugs to numb an area you are going to train or break with. Stay in tune with your body at all times. If you are training with a partner, do not let his progress influence the intensity of your training, beyond drawing a little courage to endure the pain. Be aware of how much pain you are taking; too much courage will reverse what progress you have made.

Summarily, Pyrrhonian reasoning teaches us that how hard we strike targets in the initial stages of training must be determined by the individual who is training, not by on-lookers or in terms of pounds per square inch. It teaches us that no two bodies will start with the same strength or progress at the same rate. If your training partner is punching through four inches of wood in six months and you are not yet able to hit your training block with full power, do not attempt to keep up with him. This is how injuries occur. Let your body do its job in making the adjustments to the demand you are placing on it, and let it do so at its own pace. This point cannot be stressed enough, and as we go on now to the study of reaction forces by the theory of Sir Isaac Newton, the accompanying graphic illustrations should further caution you on pushing too hard in your training and give you a good understanding of exactly what happens when an accelerated body weapon makes contact with a target.

The physicist Sir Isaac Newton needs no formal introduction. His teachings and theories are taught in American schools at the elementary level. Of particular interest to us here and now is his third law of motion that states concisely that for every action there is an equal and opposite reaction. What this means to us is that if we emit a thousand pounds of impact force with a punch and make contact with a target, there will be a thousand pounds of reaction force either coming back into the hand or passing through the target if it cannot resist the pressure. Observe Figure 1: "A" is the sending force of "B," the weapon, which is on its way to "C," the target. "A" would be the practitioner and "B" could be a punch, for example. Following Figures 1, 2, and 3, you will observe the weapon following its course toward the target until its impact in Figure 3. At the point in Figure 1 at which the weapon has just left the chamber position, the inertial resistance puts a drain on the speed of the weapon because the weapon was not moving before this point. By the time the weapon has reached the position in Figure 2, the speed

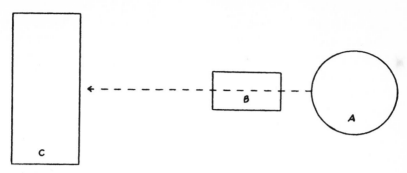

Figure 1

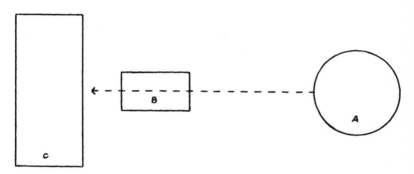

Figure 2

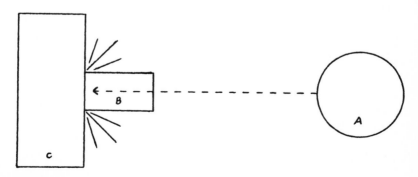

Figure 3

will have greatly increased. The same force propelling the weapon toward the target will have greater effect on the weapon because it is already moving, requiring less effort to move it along its course. At the point of impact illustrated in Figure 3, the weapon will have reached its greatest speed. It will have steadily increased in velocity from the effort being placed into the movement, and the locking technique and snapping motion of the punch will also increase the speed at this point, but here is where reaction forces come into play. Up until the point of impact, most of the forces against the weapon have been positive and propelling it in the same direction. Upon impact, however, the weapon will encounter increased negative reaction force resisting the positive effort. It is at this point that positive and negative reaction forces begin passing through the weapon and through the target. If the density of the weapon and the applied velocity are not strong enough to pass through the target, the majority of the reaction forces will return to the weapon, less the amount that the target is able to absorb without breaking. If the weapon passes through the target, the opposite will occur. Whether or not the weapon passes through the target, however, a percentage of the reaction forces will pass through the weapon. When you are conditioning your weapon for breaking, you are first training it to increase its strength and density to be able to pass through the target without damage to the weapon. You are also training it to resist and withstand the negative reaction forces that will always be present in breaking. The more easily the weapon overcomes the target, the lesser the percentage of negative reaction force. Look at Figure 4, which shows the target being contacted by the weapon. The large black arrows marked positive and negative in circles at their tips denote the force of the weapon (positive), and the resistance force of the target (negative). When these two forces meet, the reactions denoted by the thin arrows and marked with the hexagons at their tips occur. The negative reaction force returns to the weapon; the positive reaction force continues through the target. If the density of the target and the weapon are the same, and the

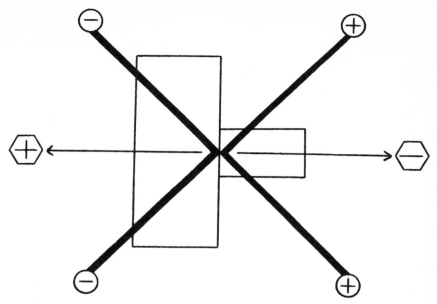

Figure 4

speed applied to the weapon is not sufficient to cause the
target to break, both the target and the weapon will absorb
an equal amount of reaction force. Two objects of equal
density colliding will evenly share the "equal and opposite
reaction." When speed is applied to the weapon, however,
in an amount that will cause it to overcome the density of
the target, and thereby breaking it, the greater portion of the
reaction from the contact is expelled in positive force. This
is, of course, theoretical and subject to variables according
to Pyrrhonian standards, but experience has dictated that
much greater pain, if any at all, will be felt from an unsuccessful breaking attempt than from a successful one.

What all this teaches is that a full-speed blow should always
be applied in breaking attempts. Where there is a lack of
confidence, hesitation at the last moment may cause you to
pull your strike or slow it down at impact. Just as an improperly delivered or focused blow can cause damage to the
weapon, a blow that is pulled at the last moment for the lack
of confidence can also cause damage, or at least an undue
amount of pain. File the illustration in Figure 4 in the back
of your mind to refer to when you make your first breaking

attempt. You should be able to strike the object you are going to attempt to break with full power several times on a flat supported surface before attempting to break it. From this you will gain confidence that you will not be injured in the breaking attempt. If you have confidence that you will not hurt yourself when you contact the target with a full-power blow, you will not hesitate at the last moment or pull your power or speed. These reaction forces will be discussed again in Chapter Four with respect to the direction they will pass through the weapon, and what other areas of the body will be affected by these forces. Bearing in mind what has been discussed here, a careful study of Chapter Four would be wise before you begin any training.

Chapter 2

Anatomical Weapons of the Hand

The four most crucial weapons of the hand are the punch, backhand, suto, and palm, and it is these four weapons that will be studied in this chapter. These four strokes provide an array of striking angles at both long and short distances, and are the most devastating in terms of impact force. These are the strikes that are most likely to be used in a combative situation. Unless you have trained yourself specifically to respond with other hand strikes, it will be one of these that you will use in a reflex response, be it offense or defense.

PUNCH AND BACKHAND

Figure 5 is an overhead view of the skeletal structure of the left hand. The middle and index finger are detached, and the area enclosed by the oblong box is the area that makes the actual contact when using a straight punch or a backhand strike. They are the tips of the bones of the top of the hand. When the fist is formed, the fingers are rolled downward, exposing the area. It is this area that makes the contact, and this area that must be strengthened. Figure 6 is a head-on view of the fist with the proper area of contact noted (see also Figure 7). Form your hand into a fist and observe that

11

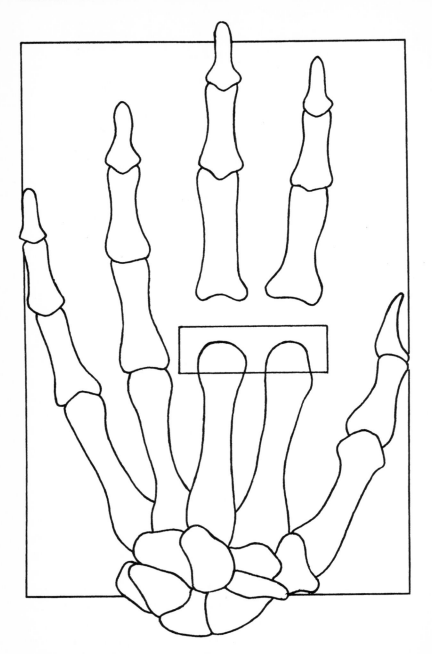

Figure 5

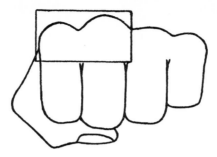

Figure 6

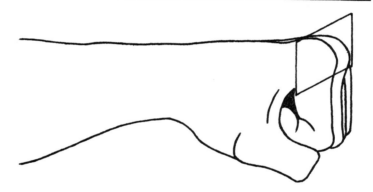

Figure 7

when this is held in a normal alignment with the forearm, only the middle knuckle would make contact with a target, along with the corresponding finger. Proper alignment will call for two adjustments. Looking back at Figure 7, note that the top of the hand is held level with the top of the forearm. If you laid it against a wall, the forearm, wrist, and fist would all be touching the wall simultaneously. This position gives the bones of the hand a perfect structural alignment with the bones of the forearm, and thus alleviates the greatest possible amount of give at the wrist joint, protecting it from sprain and maximizing resistance to negative impact force. The second adjustment that must be made is to rotate the fist slightly to the outside to allow the first and second

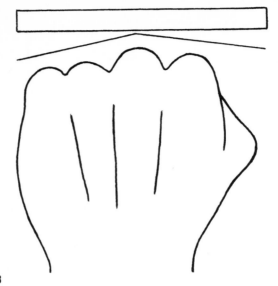

Figure 8

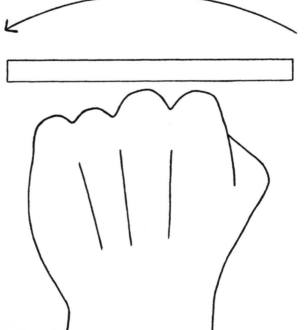

Figure 9

knuckle to strike the target surface simultaneously. Figure 8 demonstrates how the middle knuckle protrudes further than the others, requiring the rotation noted in Figure 9. Rotate the hand only as much as is necessary to compensate for the protrusion and produce a surface that will allow the first and second knuckles to contact the target together. When making this rotation, do not allow the first adjustment to be affected either upward or downward. Proper alignment is crucial to maximize power and safety to the joints.

The head-on view of the fist in Figure 10 has crossed lines at the precise area of the knuckles where the punch should be focused. Figure 10 depicts the horizontal position of the punch, but the same area is used when applying the punch

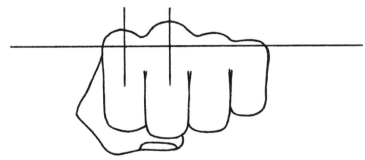

Figure 10

vertically as illustrated in Figure 11. The adjustments made at the wrist in rotating the fist to the outside and aligning the bones of the hand with the bones of the forearm are inviolable and are to be maintained in the vertical punch as well as the horizontal. A vertical punch on a target as illustrated in Figure 12 must also use only the first two knuckles. When you begin training on the practice blocks to toughen the knuckles for breaking, refer back to these illustrations as often as necessary. This alignment is a key element of power in the punch.

The backhand strike utilizes the same general area as the straight punch, but, as Figure 13 illustrates, it is the area closer to the top of the hand on the knuckles that is used

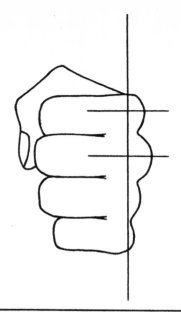

Figure 11

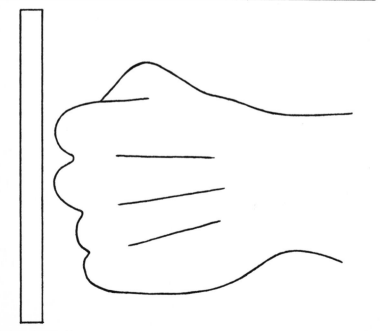

Figure 12

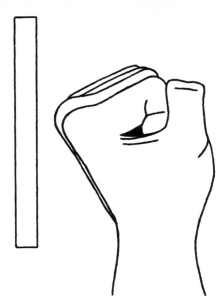

Figure 13

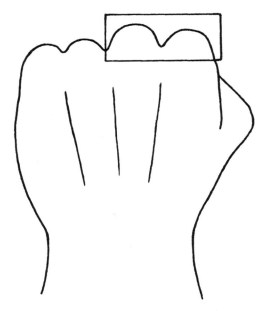

Figure 14

in this strike; therefore, the hand must be tilted at the wrist to properly form the weapon. Figure 14 denotes the proper area. Because the punch and the backhand strikes are using the same general areas, they should be trained in succession.

SUTO

The suto strike is the most versatile, most easily applied, and certainly the most devastating hand weapon on the human body. It is also the most durable and will be ready for breaking long before the other weapons of the hand. It can be applied horizontally palm-up and palm-down, vertically downward, and at an angle in a downstroke. In its full open form, it can draw power from the heel of the supporting leg and knee, the hip and shoulder, the elbow, and from centrifugal force all at the same time. Furthermore, it does not have a limited range of penetration like the punch does. Penetration can range from four inches to four feet according to the stroke used. By making a mistake, however, you can permanently damage the communicating areas of the hand very easily; therefore, the strictest attention must be paid to the proper area of this weapon.

Figure 15 is a palm-side view of the skeletal structure of the left hand denoting the proper area of contact. Following the arrows, you will see that although the wrist is in fact a weak area, when used in the proper fashion the suto strike has a great deal of structural backup behind it by approaching the wrist from the side. The actual contact area of the suto is very small, as depicted in Figure 16. The entire side of the hand is not used. The supporting bone in the top of the hand communicating with the pinkie finger is extremely fragile and sensitive to pain. At its base as it meets the bones of the wrist it widens and is strong, but any contact above the upper arrow will cause a great deal of pain and is likely to cause fracture if used against a hard surface. Figure 16 depicts the suto hand in the palm-down position, while Figures 17 and 18 depict a vertical suto. As Figure 17 illustrates, the area does not change when the direction of the stroke changes. Here again, a tilt in the wrist is required to

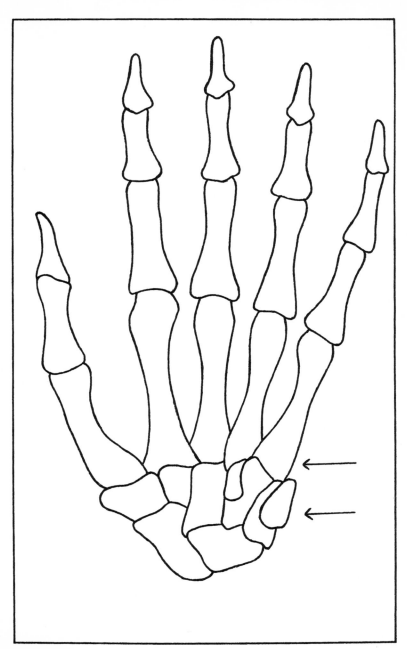

Figure 15

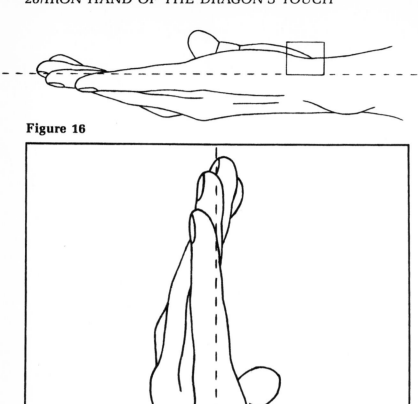

Figure 16

Figure 17

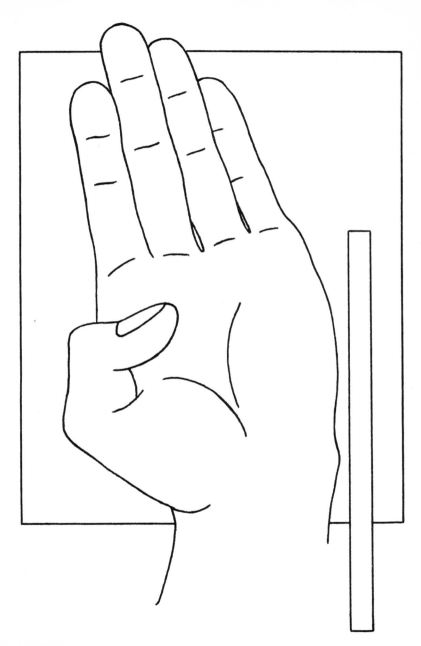

Figure 18

properly form the weapon. Note in Figure 18 that the wrist is pulled in the direction of the thumb as far as it will go. Observing Figures 16 and 17, you will note that the fingers are not locked outward. They are extended but not held perfectly straight; they are bent to lie together, but locked in the open position. Figure 18 shows the proper position of the thumb. Note that the tip of the thumb does not cross the palm of the hand to the side where the striking contact will be made. It is left on the thumb side of the hand and simply pulled downward as far as it will go. Figure 19 illustrates a suto hand formed for the palm-up position.

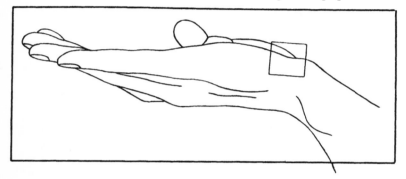

Figure 19

Carefully observe the striking area depicted, and go back to Figures 16 and 17. Looking from a side view, note that the hand has a dotted line splitting it in half, and that it is the palm-side half of the hand that is making the contact. Never make contact above this line or to the side closest to the top of the hand. Going back to the skeletal view, the small bone protruding is the pisiform bone. With your index finger, push on the pisiform bone, and roll the finger against it until the fingernail touches the skin. This is all the area that is used in the suto strike. Go to Figures 20 and 21. These both depict a horizontal suto strike whose stroke originated from the thumb-side direction. Figure 20 is a palm-up strike, Figure 21 a palm-down strike. Note that both are tilted to the palm side of the hand. Observing once again Figures 16 and 17, note

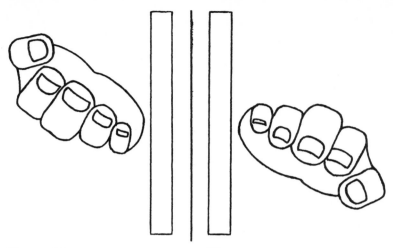

Figure 20   **Figure 21**

that the palm side of the hand is the proper striking area. If you look at either Figure 20 or 21 with the target facing your lap instead of to your right or left, you will observe the proper angle for a downward suto strike. Again, the contact is being made at the palm side of the hand. Familiarize yourself with this area; in your practice on the blocks, train your hands to form this tilt automatically and without thought.

Figure 22 depicts the hand formed for a suto in a way that would be formed by someone who has injured the pinkie

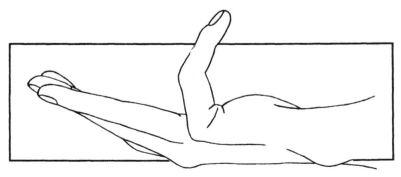

Figure 22

bone in the side of the hand from improperly forming the suto and striking a hard surface. They will be trying to flex the small muscle in the side of the hand that runs along the pinkie bone trying to protect it, and understandably so: it hurts to hit it on a hard surface. Save yourself this painful experience with the conditioning process you are about to engage in. Be sure you are hitting the proper area of the hand.

PALM

If you will look back at Figure 15 and then at Figure 23, you will notice the close proximity on the hand that is being used for the suto and the palm strike. Like the punch and backhand therefore, the suto and palm should be trained in succession.

Referring to Figure 23, the group of bones enclosed by the box is the proper area of contact. Figure 24 shows a surface view of the right hand with the contact area noted. The entire palm area is not used, and because the area is limited in terms of contact surface, a tilt of the hand is again necessary. Observe Figure 25. The hand is rotated to the pinkie side just far enough to keep the thumb side of the hand from making contact. Figure 26 shows a head-on view of the right hand making contact with a target, illustrating the tilt at the wrist. Note that the hand and fingers are held loosely. Spread the fingers comfortably and leave the thumbs open. Do not lock the thumb down as was done in forming the suto hand.

As noted in the suto area description, this area of the hand is dense and strong. The palm strike, therefore, like the suto, will condition quickly and be ready for breaking long before the punch or backhand strikes.

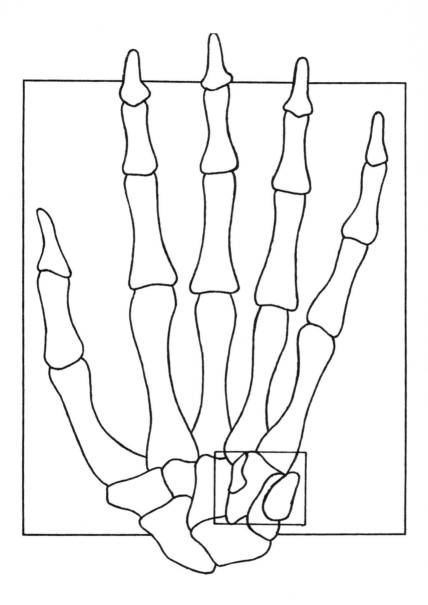

Figure 23

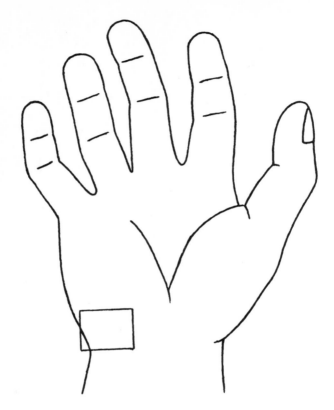

Figure 24

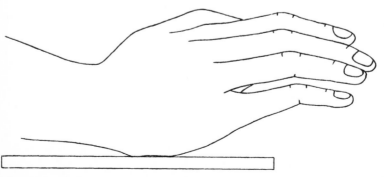

Figure 25

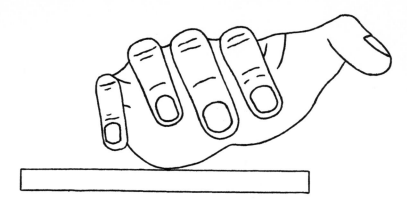

Figure 26

Chapter 3

Anatomical Weapons of the Feet

In this chapter we are going to study the three anatomical weapons of the feet that are most often used in breaking techniques. These three are the most useful in a combative situation as well. You will also find that within these three kicks you will have covered the majority of kicking contact areas applied in most styles of kung-fu and karate in the various other kicks.

Just as angles and concentration points were important factors in applying the weapons of the hand, those same factors are of equal importance here. There are fragile areas on the foot very close to the areas that you will be developing for breaking, so as in the study of hand weapons, care should be taken in locating the areas on your own body and using them properly and accurately.

FRONT KICK

Figure 27 is a skeletal illustration of the right foot. There is a dotted line passing through the illustration, and there is a black arrow showing an angle of approximately twelve degrees. The dotted line illustrates the ideal angle for the negative impact force to pass through the foot. The black arrow illustrates the most common direction that this

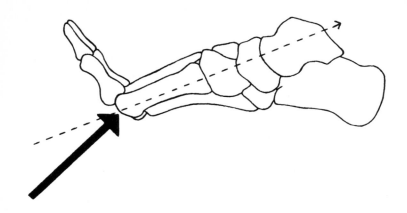

Figure 27

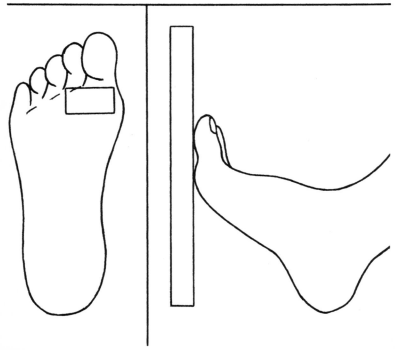

Figure 28   **Figure 29**

reaction force will pass through the foot. Figure 28 shows the precise area of contact on a target when using the front kick. In Figure 29, the right foot is shown against a target as it will typically make the contact. Because the knee is the fulcrum point of the kick, where the knee is (in relation to the height of the target) will determine exactly how much the toes are required to bend backward. The toes must be pulled back as far as they will go as the kick is delivered. At the angle depicted by Figure 29, the toes will be safe from injury on contact with the target regardless of its strength. This target is at a ninety-degree angle with the floor. In Figure 30, the target is parallel with the floor as it would be in practicing an overhead break with the front kick. The toes are bent back considerably further, but this is not the result of a controlled effort. If you were breaking an overhead object with the front kick, the toes would probably contact the target first and be pushed out of the way as the kick continued toward the target and finally made full contact. At times a mild sprain will occur when the toes are forced back this

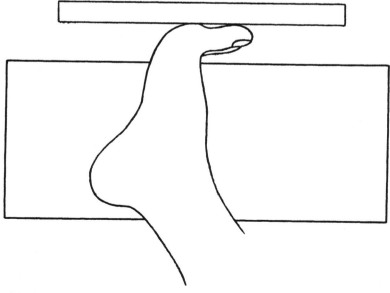

Figure 30

far, but in time the ligaments will stretch, allowing the toes to bend back this far without strain. If you have trouble getting your toes back, it would be wise to stretch them back with your hands or by kneeling on the floor with your toes bent and the ball of the foot resting on the floor. Gently apply pressure to the toes to loosen the joints. If you thrust a front kick out and hit a firm target with your toes not pulled back, they would more than likely be broken. Keep your toes pulled back at all times when delivering this kick.

HOOK KICK

A hook kick applied in sparring is often executed by making a slapping-type contact with the ball end of the foot or with the entire bottom of the foot landing flush. The hook kick as applied in a combative situation is the same type that will be studied here as a breaking weapon. Observe Figure 31, a skeletal illustration of the right foot with two areas noted. The area pointed to by the black arrow is the proper area of contact for the hook kick. The area sectioned off by the

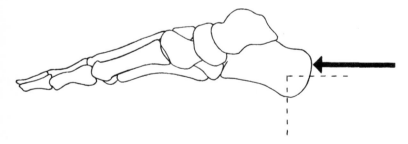

Figure 31

dotted ninety-degree angle is the area that you will never forget striking a hard target with if you are unfortunate enough to make the mistake. Figure 32 shows the direction that the negative reaction force will pass through the foot as noted by the dotted line. Precisely where the dotted line enters the foot is where the contact with the target should be made. Figure 33 is a rear-angle view of the foot, with the exact area of contact depicted by cross lines. In Figure 34

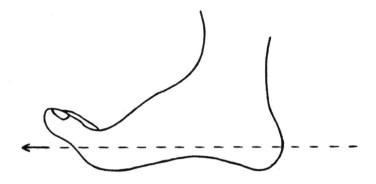

Figure 32

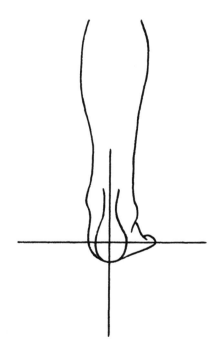

Figure 33

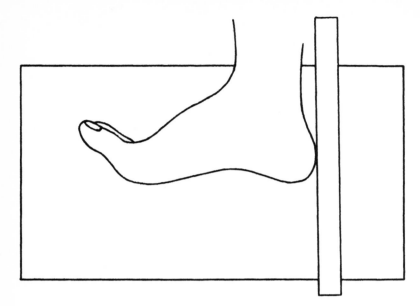

Figure 34

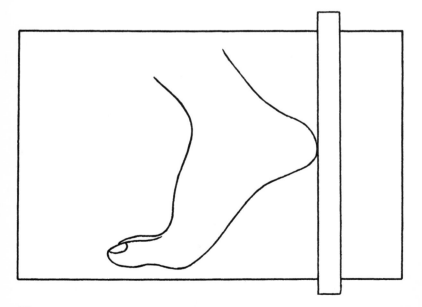

Figure 35

the foot is shown striking a target at the proper angle. The very back of the heel at its highest point is the contact area. Look now at Figure 35. This is an improperly executed hook kick. It is making contact with the point of the heel. The first time you hit a target with your heel at this angle will most likely be the last, because you will remember that pain for a long time. The point of the heel is extremely sensitive to contact with hard objects. Go back to Figure 31 and observe once again the area sectioned off by the dotted line. Do not make contact with this area on any hard object. Any anatomical targets below the bony part of the head are soft enough to strike with the point of the heel, excluding joints, but contact to the head, knees, elbows, hip girdle, or any other hard object will cause extreme pain to the heel. It is best to break any habit of using the point of the heel in this kick. Study this weapon carefully before beginning any training on practice blocks. Injury to this area could take as long as six months to heal.

SIDE KICK

Because the side kick applies an area very close to the area used in the hook kick, and specifically the danger area of the heel, look back now again at Figure 31. Pay close attention to the area sectioned off by the ninety-degree dotted lines. Look now at Figure 36. The area within the dotted lines here is your weapon area. The most critical area of danger in the side kick is that area pointed to by the black arrow. Locate this area on your foot. The point of this bone runs right along the edge of the foot that you will be training and applying in breaking. You must avoid hitting this area at all costs. This bone will chip or break if it strikes a hard object, and without a great deal of pressure. Look now at Figure 37. Note the contact area shown as being the final edge on the heel end of the foot. The dotted arrow depicts the direction that the negative reaction force will pass through the foot. Look now at Figure 38. Note that there is a small portion of the bottom of the heel being used in the kick. This area is heavily protected and misses the bottom area of the heel bone. Figure

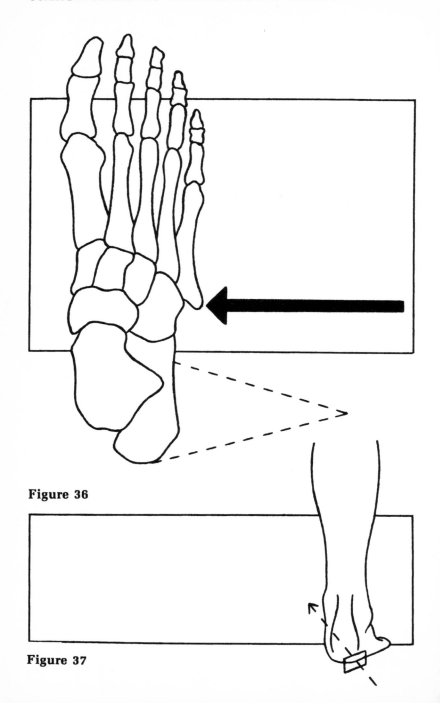

Figure 36

Figure 37

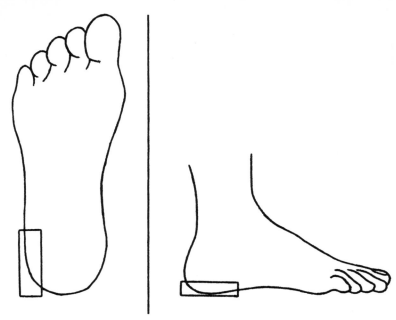

Figure 38   **Figure 39**

39 shows the outer view of the right foot with the contact area for the side kick enclosed. Look closely now at Figures 40 and 41. Figure 40 illustrates a properly executed side kick making contact with a target, while Figure 41 shows the kick landing improperly. Note in Figure 40 that the ankle is bent

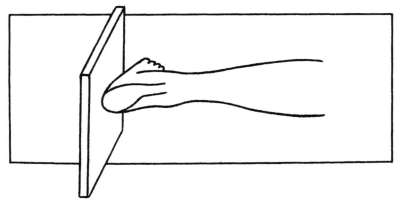

Figure 40

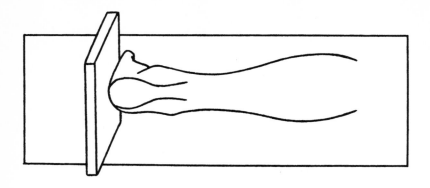

Figure 41

downward where in Figure 41 it is held straight. Note also that in Figure 40 the ankle is pulled back slightly, while in Figure 41 the ankle is holding the foot at a perfect ninety-degree angle to the lower leg. You must not strike the bottom of the heel on a hard object as it could result in injury that would require corrective surgery. If you are wearing a shoe while fighting, you can use the bottom of the heel. Barefoot application of the side kick will require proper positioning as depicted in Figure 40.

Chapter 4

Anatomical Weapons and Reaction Areas

In Chapter One we discussed positive and negative impact forces, illustrating how they interact with the weapon and with the target. We will go one step further here. We will show how negative impact force continues passing from the point of impact through the weapon until it has been absorbed. This shock in a punch, for example, can be felt in the shoulder, abdomen, and even in the heel of the rear leg, according to how great the returning force is. As this returning force passes through the weapon, it will be seeking a weak area in the arm or leg from which to escape, and will either find such an area or continue traveling through the body until it is diminished through absorption. The term *escape* as intended here does not mean to harmlessly pass away; it means that the shock would be spent in consuming a bone or a joint. It is highly unlikely that a bone in the arm or leg would crack or break under this pressure, being that the joints are weaker. Therefore, Chapter Four will include a study of the major joints that will be affected by the shock.

Figure 42 is an illustration of an extended punch. When this punch contacts its target, the first reaction is felt in the weapon itself. Following the initial shock, however, the reac-

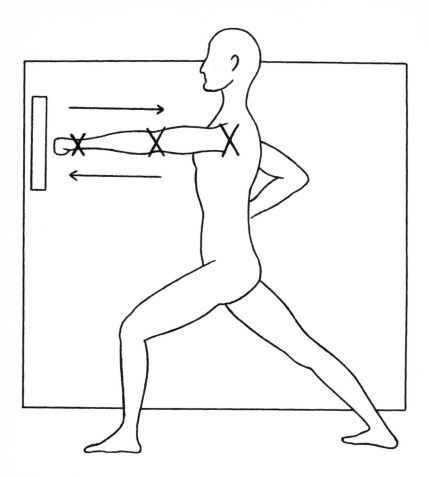

Figure 42

tion force will continue to travel through the weapon into
the wrist, the elbow, and into the shoulder. For the straight-
line punch, these three areas (marked by an X) are the major
weak areas that will be affected by the returning force.

Figure 43 is an illustration of an extended backhand strike.
Note the direction of the arrows. Because the body is not
behind the weapon, the majority of the returning force is
spent passing through the weapon itself. There is shock to
the wrist but, as a rule, there will be no shock felt in other

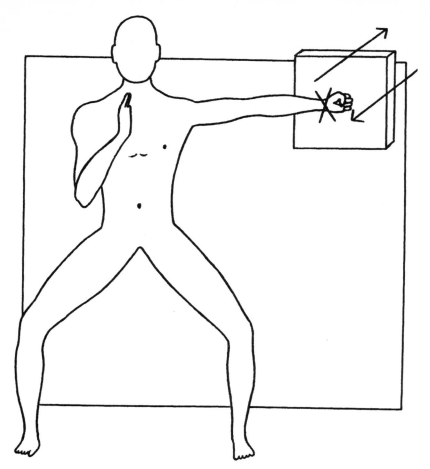

Figure 43

areas of the body unless the strike has been improperly
delivered.

Observe now Figures 44 and 45. Figure 44 is a vertical suto,
and 45 is a vertical palm. The final six inches of these two
strikes are very similar, and the extended arm in Figure 45
would not be an incorrect position for the suto, nor would
the bent arm in Figure 44 be incorrect in applying the palm.
The positioning of the elbow in these two strikes structurally
controls the depth of the strokes. For both the vertical suto

Figure 44

and the vertical palm, therefore, a bent arm application would confine the shock to the wrist, whereas the extended arm application would allow the shock to pass on into the elbow. The X indicates the affected areas.

Figure 46 illustrates a front kick in the fully opened position. The arrows indicate the typical path for the positive and negative reaction forces to travel. The most affected areas for this stroke are again noted by the X. The kick illustrated is at hip level. When the front kick is used above the waist,

Figure 45

the shock will also pass through the hip. If you look back now at Figure 42, taking notice of the arrows denoting the positive and negative impact forces, and then look at the arrows in Figure 46 comparing the number of joints involved in the reaction process, you will see that the more solid the backup structure of the stroke is, the greater the amount and distance of the shock to the body.

Figure 47 illustrates an extended hook kick. The shock for this movement will be restricted to the ankle and to the knee

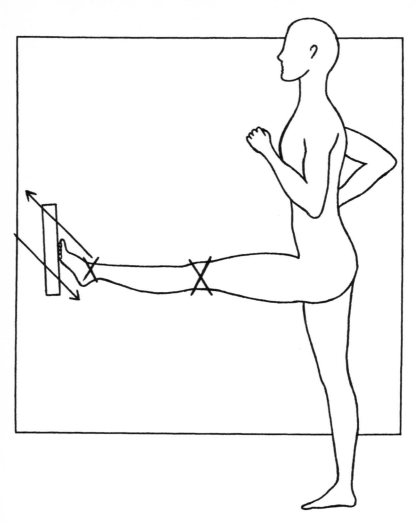

Figure 46

as indicated by the X markings.

In Figure 48 the side kick is illustrated with the major joints receiving a reaction to the negative impact force denoted. Once again, go back to Figure 42 and observe that illustration, comparing it to this one. Both the side kick and the straight-line punch are thrusts involving strokes of limited penetra-

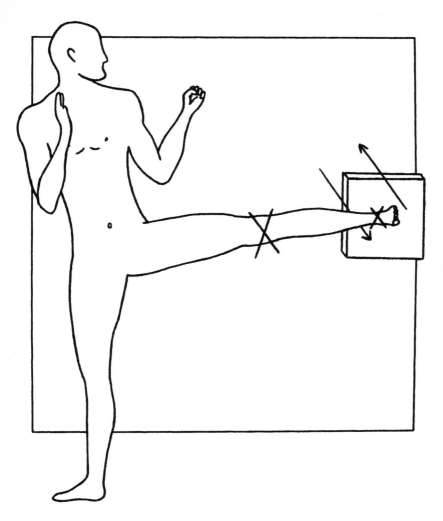

Figure 47

tion. At their extended points, both have the body structure
behind them. The other five strokes illustrated here draw
power from centrifugal force involving an arc in the movement. At their extended points, the body is *not* behind the
weapon. What is noteworthy to remember here is that the
straight-line punch and the side kick, both being thrust

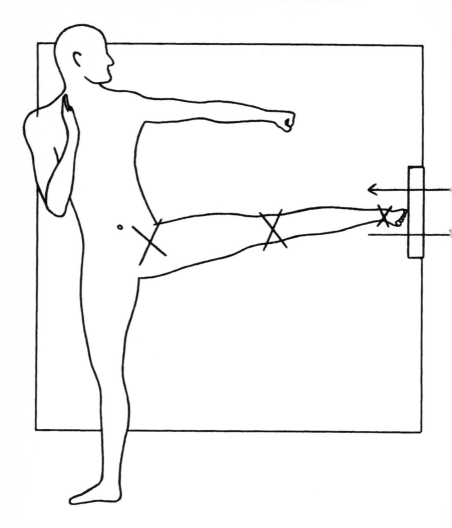

Figure 48

movements and having the body structure behind them, are in fact limited as far as depth and penetration, but they are more solid than the other five and are able to emit a force that is less likely to be resisted by a target, because more muscle and body weight are behind both. These two strokes, because they are shorter, will also be quicker in terms of the time it takes for the weapon to leave the body's chamber position and reach its target. The centrifugal force blows will have amassed greater speed by the time they contact the target, but because they involve a longer stroke, the time it takes for the blow to reach the target will also be greater.

STRENGTHENING REACTION AREAS

We just learned that the reaction to negative impact force as discussed in Chapter One will go beyond the anatomical weapon and reach into other areas of the body. Now we will study how to strengthen these areas with rather simple but important exercises. These exercises will be numbered, and in the chapter giving the training process they will be referred to and be an integral portion of the routine.

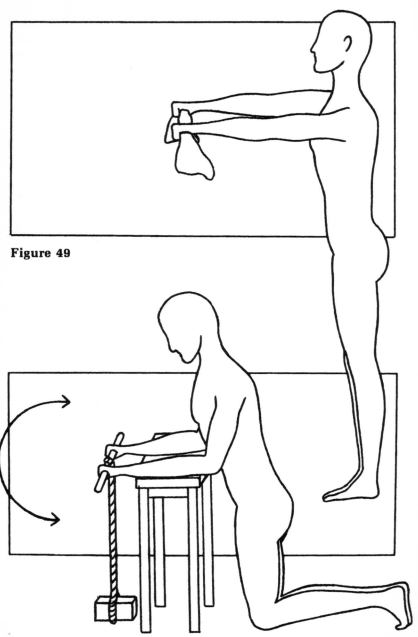

Figure 49

Figure 50

Exercise #1

In Figure 49, a towel is being held at arm's length. By squeezing the towel as hard as you can and then releasing it, you are exercising the muscles that control the hand, fingers, and wrist. A strong forearm will give power to the wrist and hands, strengthening both for breaking and other uses as well.

Exercises #2 and #3

In Figure 50, a brick is tied to a stick for resistance, and the wrists are to follow the arc as depicted by the arrow. Relax the wrists, allowing them to bend downward as far as they will go, then pull them upward as far as they will go. This exercise will further strengthen the wrists and forearms. The palm-down position depicted in Figure 50 is exercise #2. To perform exercise #3, reverse the grip on the stick, holding the palms facing upward with the tops of the forearms resting on the table. Follow the same arc of the movement. Exercise #2 strengthens the wrist and top of the forearm, while exercise #3 strengthens the inside of the forearm and the wrist.

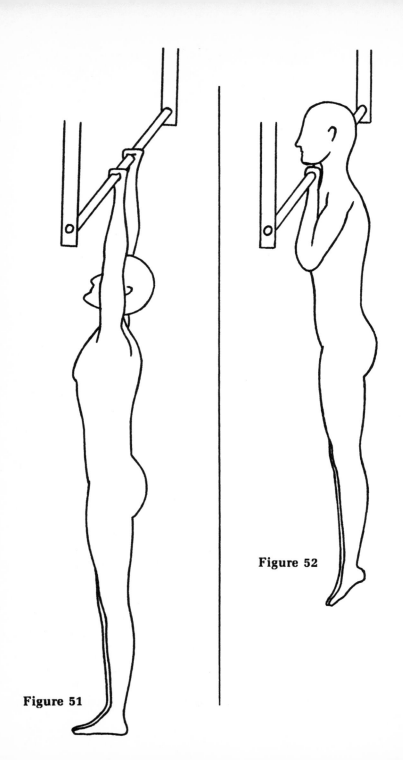

Figure 51

Figure 52

Exercises #4 and #5

The illustrations in Figures 51 and 52 depict the positions for the fourth and fifth exercises. Exercise #4 is the pull-up, executed by pulling the chin up to the bar, palms facing away from the body. To position yourself for exercise #5, simply grip the bar with the palms facing you instead of away from you, again pulling your body up until the chin reaches the bar. Exercise #4 strengthens the lats, shoulder blades, and sides of the shoulder caps. Exercise #5 works essentially the same areas but includes the biceps as well.

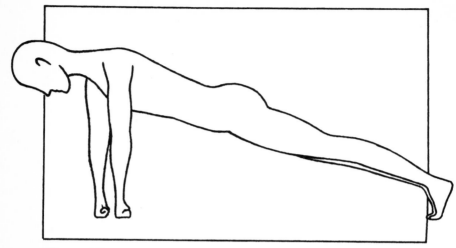

Figure 53

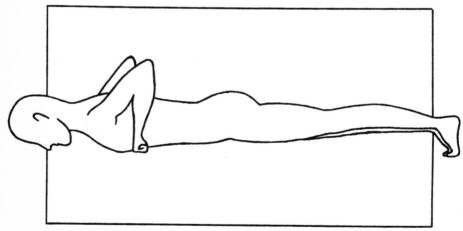

Figure 54

Exercise #6

Depicted by Figures 53 and 54, the push-up strengthens a variety of muscles in the upper body. When performed on a closed fist as illustrated here instead of on the palms, the wrist is also strengthened. The elbows should be held close to the body during the entire exercise.

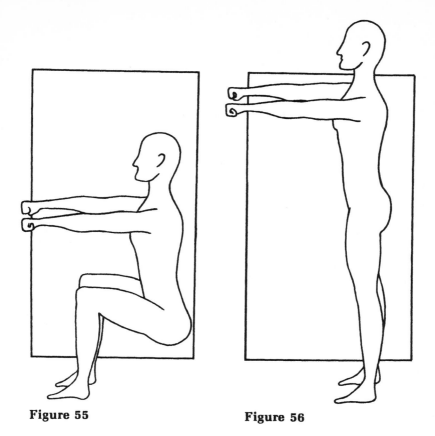

Figure 55   **Figure 56**

Exercises #7 and #8

Here we begin working the muscles of the lower body. In exercise #7, the feet will be positioned under the shoulders as depicted by Figure 55. Exercise #8 requires a wider stance, at least six inches beyond the span of the shoulders. To perform the movement, squat at the knee joint just far enough to break the parallel plane between the upper leg and the floor (Figure 56), and return to the standing position. It is important to break the parallel plane to bring the buttocks thoroughly into play in the movement. These two exercises are going to strengthen the quadriceps, femoral biceps, and buttocks, all of which will increase the power output of your kicks and strengthen the reaction areas affected by negative impact force. If necessary, use a chair or other object to maintain your balance during the exercise.

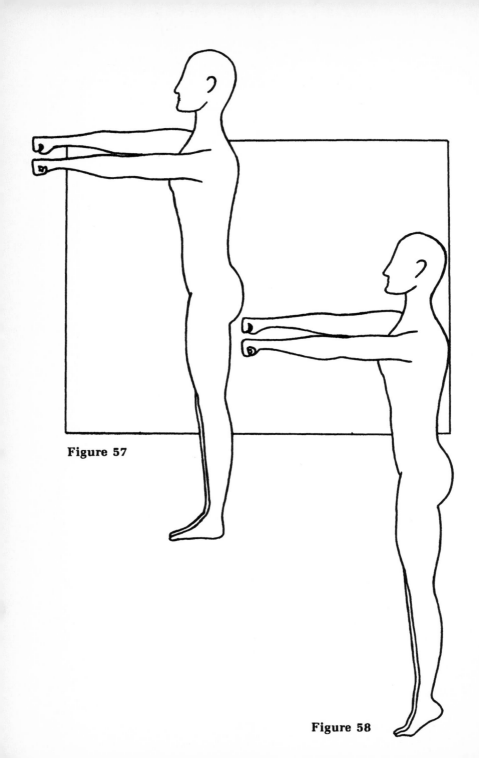

Figure 57

Figure 58

Exercise #9

In Figures 57 and 58, the simple exercise illustrated will greatly strengthen the calf muscles, which play an important role in ankle strength and movement. With the feet held together, simply extend the ankles downward, raising the body up and on the balls of the feet. Again, a chair or wall may be used to maintain balance.

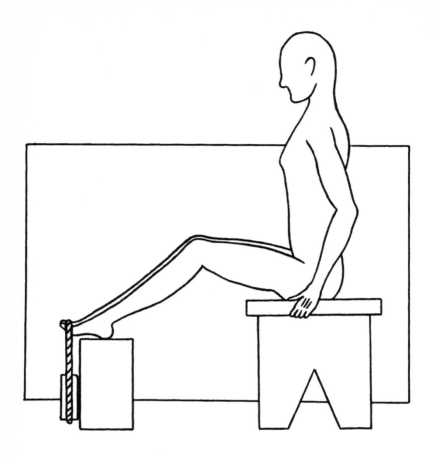

Figure 59

Exercise #10

Figures 59 and 60 illustrate the final exercise. A brick, used here for resistance, is tied to a rope and held in the crook of the toes. Extend the ankles forward as far as they will go, then draw them upward as far as they will go. The tiny muscles in the foot and around the ankle, and the muscles around the shin bone are being worked in this movement. As the ankle will receive a shock in all kicking techniques,

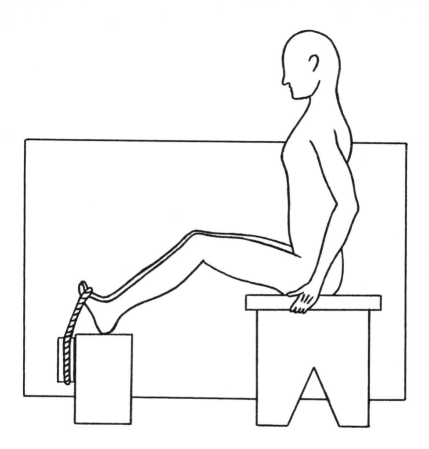

Figure 60

it is important to strengthen the area as much as possible.

The number of sets and repetitions for each of these exercises will be given in the chapter covering the training process. Perform these exercises slowly and always use the maximum range of movement of each. It is as important to have your muscular power up to par in breaking as it is to have the contact areas conditioned. Do not shortcut on this area of training.

Chapter 5

Construction of Training Blocks

We have thus far discussed positive and negative reaction forces, the anatomy of hand and foot weapons, where reaction forces will be felt in the body, and how to strengthen the respective areas. Having come this far, we will now discuss training blocks and how they may be constructed.

Figure 61 is a typical example of a hand-held practice block. It can be held on the floor with one hand and struck

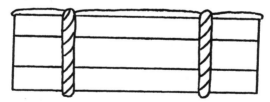

Figure 61

with the other, or held vertically by a training partner. This training block is composed of two pieces of rope approximately twenty-four inches long, a piece of burlap-backed carpet about six by twelve inches, two one-inch boards measuring six by twelve inches, and a piece of foam rubber also measuring six by twelve inches. Figure 62 is an exploded diagram of the hand-held training block. At the very top is

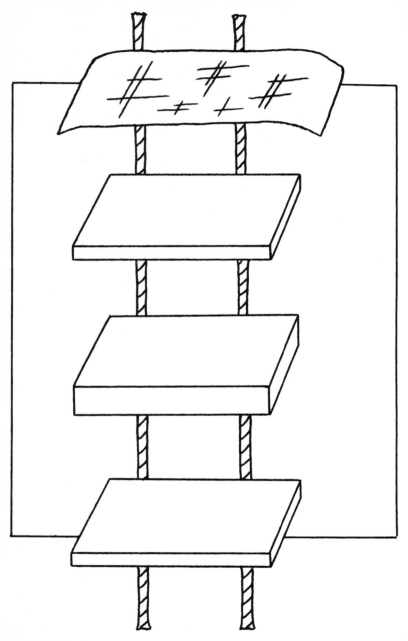

Figure 62

a piece of burlap-backed carpet faced with the burlap side outward. Burlap is a very coarse material and will be hard on the skin, causing tiny cuts which will begin building a surface callous. Under the section of carpet is a six-by-twelve board to make the striking surface rigid. Under that board is a piece of foam rubber followed by another board, all measuring the same, six by twelve. The foam between the two boards allows the striking block to give against the pressure of the blows. In time, as the hands and feet grow used to the block and can be hit at full power, the density of the target can be increased by removing the foam and inserting a less pressure-absorbing material between the boards, such as three or four layers of terry cloth or some similar type of material. Once the materials are cut and ready to put together, it is best to pile them on the floor in their proper order and have someone stand on top of the pile while it is being tied. This will allow a firm binding of the ropes around the loose materials, reducing the frequency of tightening the ropes which will be needed periodically. To again increase the density of the target, simply remove the terry cloth one layer at a time until you are hitting the block with no pressure-absorbing material between the boards. Never make such an adjustment unless you are capable of hitting the block full power without pain.

Figure 63 depicts a wall-mounted striking block with the same structural features as the hand-held type. This block measures twelve by twelve inches. Figure 64 is an exploded diagram of the wall-mounted unit. To the far left is the burlap back carpet, again with the burlap faced to the striking area. A board follows, followed by a piece of foam rubber. The structure mounted to the wall should be preconstructed as one solid unit and should be put together with glue and screws. Figure 65 is a rear view of the solid section of the unit. None of these parts are to be moveable; this should be one solid section. The three-piece rear face allows the ropes to pass freely behind the unit after it is mounted to avoid having to take it down to change the burlap surface or density.

Figure 66 illustrates a floor block, which is nothing more

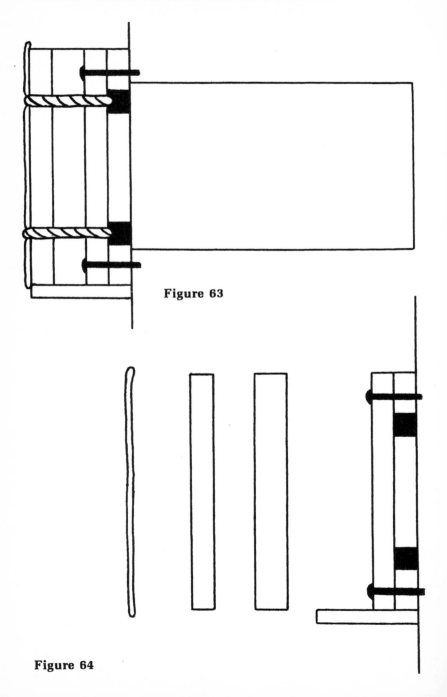

Figure 63

Figure 64

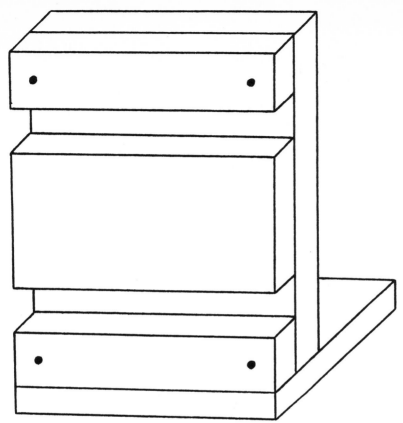

Figure 65

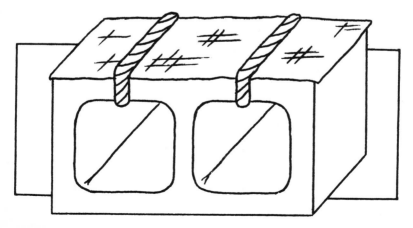

Figure 66

than a cement block with a burlap surface tied to it. Either terry cloth or foam may be laid over the block before the burlap is tied to it, but if foam is used a board will have to be laid over it to make the surface rigid enough to be beneficial for training.

Chapter 6

The Training Process

We have now been through the necessary prerequisite studies to prepare you for the training process. If there is any doubt in your mind at this point about the contact areas of the anatomical weapons, stop now and go back over the material until you are satisfied that you have a full understanding of your hand and foot weapons. Every mistake you make from this point forward will be a costly one.

At this stage you will have to begin a self-study, joining fact and philosophy with trial-and-error experience. Be cautious and deliberate in your efforts to make gains in your training without injury. Combine the teaching here with that self-study; you must become your own instructor.

PUNCH

In the illustration in Figure 67, you are standing in front of the wall-mounted unit. Both hands are in the chamber position and you are in a forward stance. Measure the depth of your punch so that when it is extended you will have approximately one inch of penetration into the target. Adjust your distance from the target accordingly. When you send your punch forward, you should be using half of your power

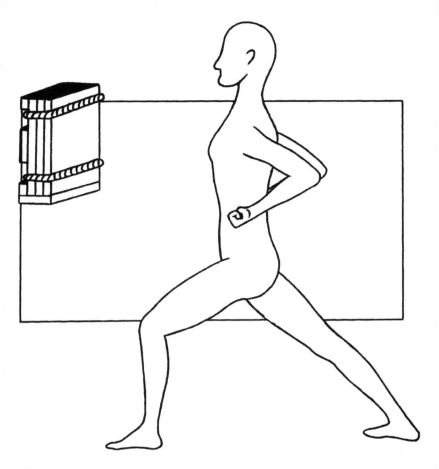

Figure 67

and half of your speed. It is important not to pull your punches; rather, extend them to the fully open position. If the target is too hard to do this, put a layer of towel under the burlap. It is better to use half power and half speed on a softer target than to use a lesser punching capacity on a hard target. Keep in mind that you are conditioning bones, muscles, and joints along with your weapon surfaces. Get in the habit of using your strikes at their proper range and extension. The technique of your strikes is of equal importance to the long-term ability in breaking.

For the exercise in Figure 68 you will be using a ten-by-four, forty-repetition formula. Here the left punch is extended into the target. The right punch will follow, then the left, and so on for a count of twenty, which will give you a total of ten repetitions on each hand. Keep your focal points in mind and adjust the movement as necessary to strike the target with the proper area of the hand. Once you have set your stance in the proper range, do not move your feet until you have completed the set of twenty repetitions. Rapid punching is taboo. One breath should be taken in and one expelled

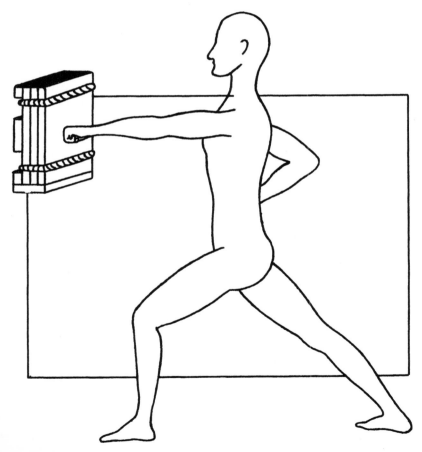

Figure 68

between each punch; these are single-stroke concentration punches.

After your first set of punches, get a towel and perform exercise #1 (see Chapter Four) for fifty repetitions, squeezing your hands in an alternating sequence until you have completed the fifty repetitions. After the training exercise on the towel, wait two minutes, return to the conditioning block, and repeat another set of twenty punches. Again perform exercise #1 for fifty repetitions, alternating the right hand with the left. Repeat the entire sequence four times until you have thrown a total of eighty punches on the block and completed two hundred repetitions on the towel. Keep a close watch on the knuckles as you are going through the punching sets. If a soft puffiness begins to develop on or around the knuckles, stop the training and go to the next phase of the hand-conditioning process. If this happens again on your next training day, wait two weeks before punching again. This is the result of the target being too hard, and it will be necessary to add two or three additional layers of padding under the burlap. This fluid buildup on the knuckles must not be permitted.

BACKHAND

In Figure 69 you are again set for training on the wall-mounted block. Your back and stance are parallel to the wall. Stand in a straddle stance, with your feet spread a little more than shoulder-width apart and your weight evenly distributed on your legs. Measure the distance and depth of your stroke to penetrate one inch into the target. Again, you are to use half power and half speed with full extension of the strike. Take one breath in and let one breath out between strikes. Always return the arm to the full chamber position as illustrated in Figure 69; do not allow the elbow to hang in the air. Figure 70 illustrates the left hand contacting the target. For the backhand, you will do ten repetitions on the left and then move to the opposite side of the target, resetting your stance to do the repetitions of the right hand. You are again on a ten-rep, four-set sequence, a total of forty repetitions on each hand. When you have completed ten repetitions on each hand, perform exercise #2 for twenty repetitions. Wait two minutes and repeat the sequence using exercise #2. Following your third and fourth sets of backhand strikes, perform exercise #3 instead of exercise #2. The striking

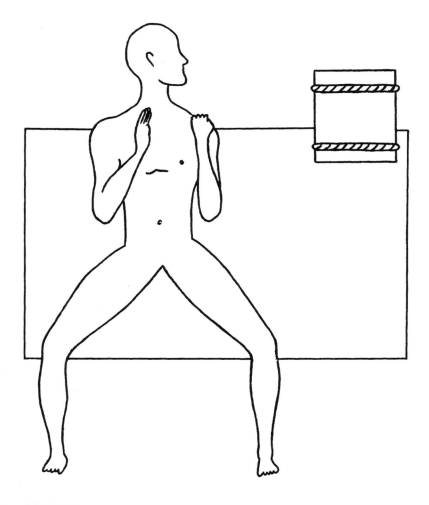

Figure 69

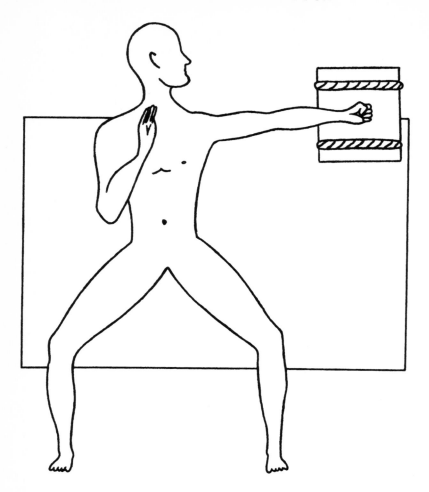

Figure 70

sequence does not change, only the exercise. Again, closely observe the knuckles during these sets. If a puffiness begins to develop, discontinue the training and go to the next hand position.

SUTO

Here the stroke is going to vary slightly. Look ahead to Chapter Seven and observe Figure 89, comparing it to

Figure 71

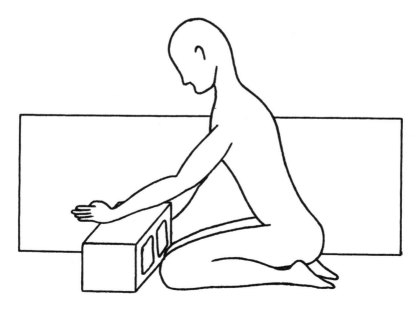

Figure 72

Figure 71 here. Because of the danger involved with an incorrectly delivered suto, as discussed in Chapter Two, the suto as practiced for conditioning should be performed from the position illustrated in Figure 71 for the first few weeks, and gradually brought closer to the chamber position at the ear. To risk damaging the side of the hand at this point for the sake of positioning would be illogical. Start from the position in Figure 71 and over a two- or three-week period, slowly raise the striking hand a little further each time you train until you reach the full chamber position at the ear. Note where the hand is in relation to the training block in Figure 72. By allowing the hand to substantially pass the center point of the block, it will be easier and safer to focus on the proper contact area for the suto.

The formula for strikes and sets does not change: four sets of ten repetitions on each hand, one breath in and one breath out between strokes, half power, half speed, gradually working your starting point in the suto up to the full chamber position. After your first and second sets, perform exercise #4. After the third and fourth sets, perform exercise #5. Sets of five to eight repetitions on both exercises will be sufficient at the start, but work your way up to sets of ten.

PALM

We're going to use the same shortened form for the palm strike as was used with the suto, and, again, the contact area on the block will be advanced forward of the center point. The leg positions illustrated for practicing the suto and the palm strikes are not mandatory. Sit comfortably, but be sure you are alert and concentrating on each strike. Four sets of ten repetitions is still the formula, with one breath in and one breath out between strikes. Exercise #6 is to be performed in numbers of repetitions that require a working of the muscles, but not to the point of exhaustion. Hold the wrist rigid during this push-up. The sequence is one set of ten repetitions on each hand as illustrated by Figures 73 and 74 on the block, and one set of exercise #6. The process is to be repeated four times until you have completed forty

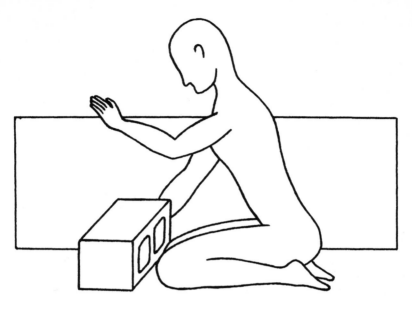

Figure 73

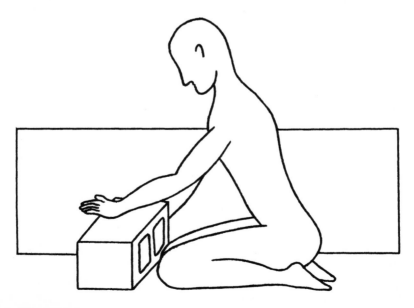

Figure 74

repetitions on the block with each hand. In your last set, and especially on the final three or four strokes, use the maximum striking force you can bear. This instruction applies to all hand strikes. Your next step in the training process will bring you some relief, but some additional discomfort as well. It is an important step in conditioning. Do not skip it.

Fill up a pot or a bucket with hot water that is large enough in which to submerge both hands simultaneously. The water should be as hot as you can stand it and should be heavily salted. Submerge your hands in the water for about five minutes, or until the water no longer feels hot to your hands. Take your hands out of the water, but do not dry them. Put a coating of dry salt directly on the areas you have trained against the block and leave it on. The salt is going to cause the skin to thicken, and the hot water is going to help heal the surface and internal areas of your weapons. Wait about one minute, add a little hot water to the bucket to compensate for the heat loss over the time that has passed since you removed your hands from the water, and submerge your salted hands back into the bucket.

Here is where you are going to find out how badly you want your hands conditioned, because after salting the striking areas, they're going to be extremely sensitive. When you submerge your hands in the water this time it's going to sting, and the sting is going to be intense for the first thirty seconds. Leave your hands submerged until the stinging stops, then remove them. Without drying your hands, salt them one more time and let them dry on their own. When your hands are dry, brush the salt off. You have finished your first day of training.

FRONT KICK

Kicks are trained separately from hand techniques, and this is day two of your training. Observe Figure 75. You are using a forward stance again, but set at a range for a front kick this time. As in the hand strikes, set your range so that the extended kick has approximately one inch of penetration into the target. In Figure 76 you have shifted your body weight onto the left leg, moving forward and locking the front kick into the target. Always return to the position in Figure 75 before throwing the next kick. Again, you will be using a ten-by-four, forty-repetition formula. Always inhale deeply and exhale before repeating a kick. When you have completed ten repetitions on one leg, change stances and throw ten kicks with the other leg. After you throw ten kicks with each leg, perform exercise #7. This exercise should be performed in sets of fifteen to twenty-five according to your individual strength. Exercise #7 should follow your first two sets of ten kicks, and exercise #8 should follow your second two sets of ten kicks. Finding the proper range for practice on the front kick will take time, and as you begin to tire, the penetration may vary. Concentration on the technique and maintaining rigidity in your form will help alleviate the problem of variation.

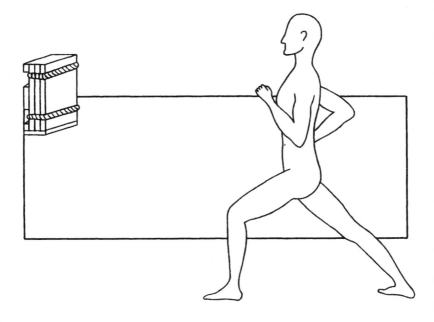

Figure 75

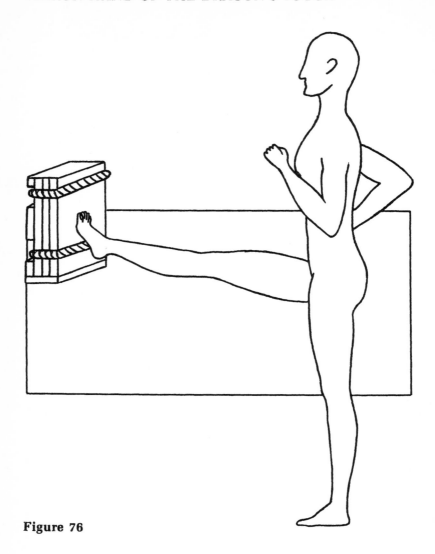

Figure 76

HOOK KICK

In Figure 77 the hook kick is depicted in its chamber position. The hook kick has two forms: the closed form, which is thrown almost like a side kick, and the wide form, which approaches its target in an arc from the chamber position shown here. The closed form is much quicker but is very

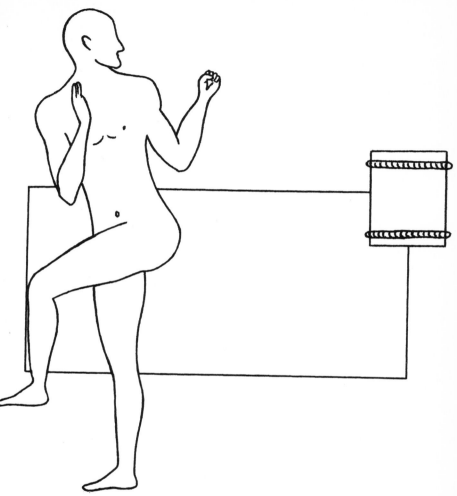

Figure 77

limited in power. The wide form is slower but its potential for power is much greater. Test your range several times before throwing the first kick of your ten-repetition set. Be sure that the extended kick lands on the proper area of the heel (Figure 78). Remember the cautions that were given in Chapter Three with regard to the point of the heel. With your range properly set, throw ten hook kicks with the left leg,

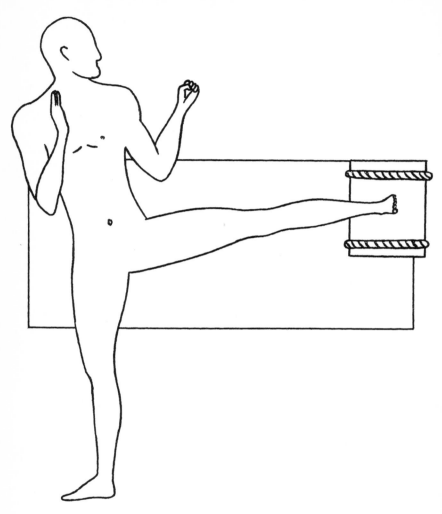

Figure 78

change stances to the opposite side of the target, and throw
ten with the right leg. It is not necessary to keep the
chambered position between kicks. Rest the foot on the floor
and chamber when you have taken your breath in and out
and are ready to throw the next kick. After you have completed ten kicks on each side, perform exercise #9 as illustrated in Figures 57 and 58 (Chapter Four). The four-set, ten-

repetition formula is also used here. The exercise will be done in sets of fifty repetitions.

SIDE KICK

The side kick will give you the greatest problems with regard to controlling the depth and resulting penetration that will be the essence of your balance. Once the side kick is locked into the fully opened position, there is no give anywhere in its structure and the negative reaction force is pushing in a straight line to the opposing hip, which will push you off balance if the kick is overpowered by the target. For this reason, you must measure your penetration and set your stance with the hip fully opened into the kick. If you measure your penetration with the leg extended but the hip not rotated into the kick, you are going to have approximately two more inches of penetration when you add your hip movement. The reaction forces have to respond to the additional penetration, which means that your kick will have to crush the target, making space for the added depth, or you will be forced backward and off balance. It will take time and practice to effectively train your side kick for breaking. In time you will develop an eye sense that will allow you to look at a target and know for which strikes you're in range. Be patient with yourself and learn from the complications you encounter.

Figure 79 shows the side kick in its chambered position. Note that the thigh is raised and held parallel to the target. The standing foot is pointed away from the target, and there should be a direct line from the heel of this foot to the exact point of contact on the target where the striking foot will land. Figure 80 illustrates the extended kick. Your sets and repetitions are again the four-by-ten, forty-repetition formula, and exercise #10 is to be performed in sets of fifteen following each set of ten right and ten left kicks. Rest the foot of the kicking leg on the floor during your breathing stops, and change the stance from right to left accordingly to train each kick. The salt-soaking procedure used for the hands should also be used on the feet.

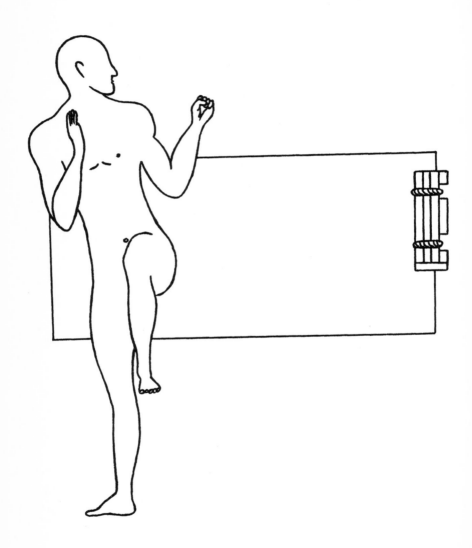

Figure 79

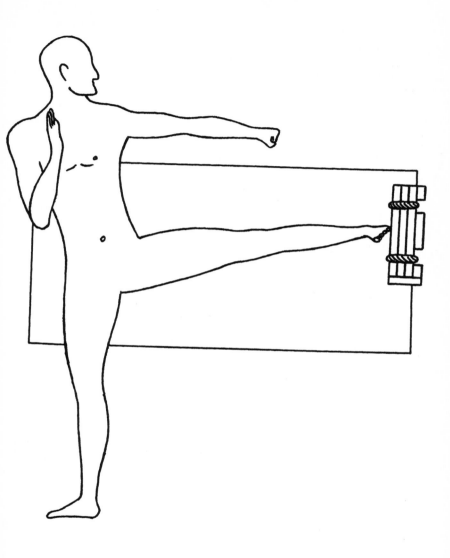

Figure 80

TRAINING SCHEDULES

The number of days you train per week may have to rely on available time. You could work a schedule such as Monday, hands; Tuesday, feet; Wednesday, rest; Thursday, hands; and Friday, feet, beginning the schedule again on Monday and taking Saturday and Sunday off. When I trained for breaking my schedule was six consecutive days, alternating hands and feet, and then one day for rest. As a rule, you will find that your first set will be the most painful. By the second set, your body will begin doing its job by shutting down the affected nerves. There will not be a complete numbness, but the difference will be noticeable. Be aware of a fluid puffiness developing on the heel of the foot during hook kicks as was advised in the punch and backhand annotations.

Chapter 7

Breaking

At this point you have seen eighty illustrations and have studied the necessary steps to prepare you for breaking. If you have trained properly and if you know you are ready to attempt your first break, then you should have already struck the boards or bricks you plan on breaking with a full-power blow without pain. If you are going to try a break on two boards with a punch, you should have already fastened the boards to your training block and hit them with a full-power blow. You should be confident that even if the boards do not break, you will not be injured from the impact. This same prerequisite should be applied to any object you plan on trying to break, whether with a weapon of the hands or the feet. Confidence is necessary; there must be no fear.

All of what you have read and seen thus far are elementary teachings from the Lian Shi kung-fu system. In this system there is a fundamental framework to all movements consisting of four elements: *Lian Li* (power), *Lian Su* (speed), *Lian Chin* (accuracy), and *Chiau Yuwn* (spirit). Power, the Lian Li element, has a physical source which comes from a trained body. Lian Su and Lian Chin also have a physical source which comes from a trained body. Chiau Yuwn means, literally, "joining the spirit," and this fourth element, which is nonphysical, must be united with the physical elements to have inner and outer unity of force in breaking or any other martial art techniques. Chiau Yuwn is difficult to teach, and I have found that it is often necessary to start a student across this bridge by giving him or her a point of focus. Not a physical point, but an emotional point. Just as many writers have been inspired to great works by the love of a mate or the tragedy of having lost one, it is helpful for the martial artist to have an emotional point of focus. To bring about anger is helpful and is a good start, but after a great many years of teaching and studying my students I have found that there is a single word and a corresponding attitude that transcends anger as a focal point. The word is *intent*. When a lioness runs down her prey and kills it, she is ferocious and purposeful in her attack, but as ferocious as she is, the lioness is not angry. She kills to eat and to feed her cubs, or for self-defense. You may one day have to fight with everything inside to survive. You would be fighting as hard and as fiercely as possible, but anger may not be present. So what would be? Intent! There would be a deliberate and purposeful desire to crush your aggressor, and not necessarily out of anger, but there would be intent. You might say that Chiau Yuwn is the will, a want channeled into the physical body but on an emotional plane, not a mental plane. What all this means in your breaking is that when you stand before the object to be broken, you must be completely committed to the task, not just physically and mentally, but emotionally as well. Your body is par for the task, and your mind has the desire to be successful in your attempt. Now you must get emotionally involved in your effort. Be it tears, a grunt, growl, or deafening scream, commit your emotions to the effort. When you add the Chiau Yuwn element to the three physical elements of Lian Li, Lian Su, and Lian Chin, you have internal as well as external powers working.

One last subject must be discussed before studying the actual breaking. Observe Figures 81 and 82. Because most of the breaking illustrations in this chapter involve a training partner holding the boards to be broken, let's take a quick

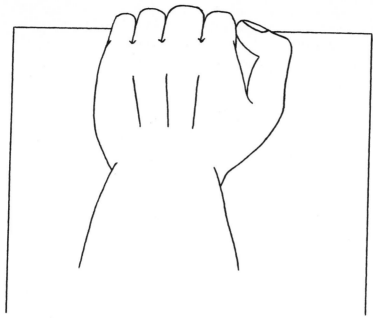

Figure 81

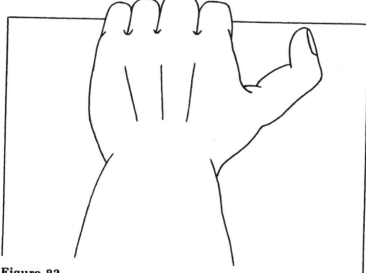

Figure 82

look at the proper way to hold the boards. A look at Figure 83 will show that the fingers are wrapped around the board on the breaking side. They should be tucked up as close to the edge of the board as possible. Look now at the position of the thumb in Figures 81 and 82. You can see here that the thumb is not involved in any way in the supportive process. Lay the thumb on the board either against the index finger as in Figure 81, or away from the rest of the hand as in Figure 82, but do not use the thumb to help hold the boards firm. The thumb can be broken or dislocated very easily, and with much less pressure it can be badly sprained. Keep the thumbs out of the way. Rest the board on the heel of the hand to keep it firm against the incoming strike. Press the board against the heel of the hand with the fingers. The thumbs are neither safe nor necessary to use in the supportive effort.

STRAIGHT PUNCH

Just as you measured off and set your stance for proximity in working on the training block, you must also measure off in breaking. An extended punch should penetrate its target by no less than two inches and up to eight inches. Observe Figures 83, 84, and 85. In Figure 83 the boards are being held at arm's length and at chest level. Never hold boards at face height. The boards will often break away from the grip and could be dangerous if they strike the face. The breaker in Figure 83 is set in a left forward stance with the left punch chambered. In Figure 84 the punch is extended to the point of contact, but notice that the arm is not locked out. In Figure 85 the punch is locked in the open position and has passed through the boards. When measuring your stance and depth of penetration, set yourself by the illustration in Figure 84. Think and decide before even setting your stance what it is you are going to do, and keep the four elements in mind. If upon impact the boards do not break and you do not feel any pain in your hand, change to a right forward stance and try again. Unless you are going for a heavy power break, it should not be necessary to support the punch with the stance, but with the opposite leg straight

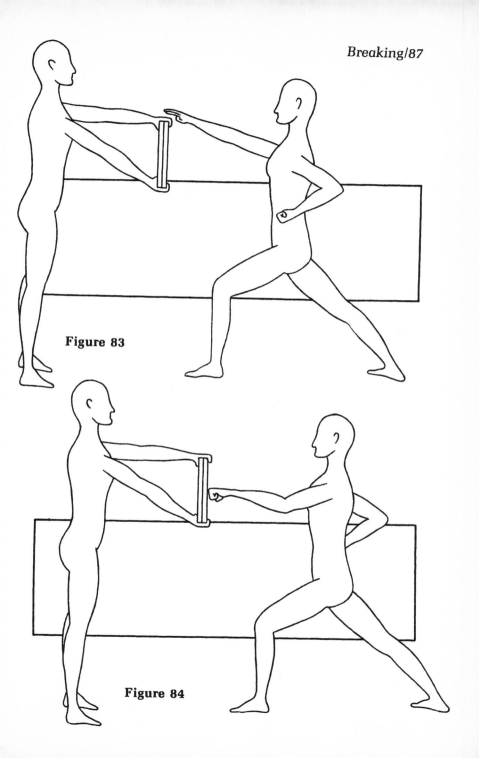

Figure 83

Figure 84

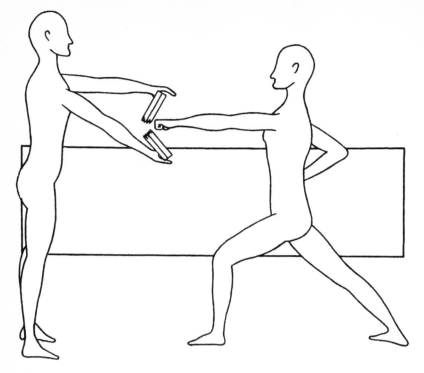

Figure 85

behind the punching arm you will have greater resistance to negative impact force and have a more solid thrust to give you more total power if needed.

BACKHAND

As you have been doing in the training process, set yourself in a straddle stance, but measure your depth for two or more inches of penetration into the boards. Looking at Figures 86, 87, and 88, you will notice that the training partner is holding the boards at a distance slightly behind the person throwing the backhand. This is necessary to keep you from striking the boards with the forearm as the knuckles make contact with the boards.

The stationary form of the backhand is strictly a speed movement and will not have nearly the power of the other hand strikes. Your expectations in terms of power therefore should not be as great when performing the backhand as

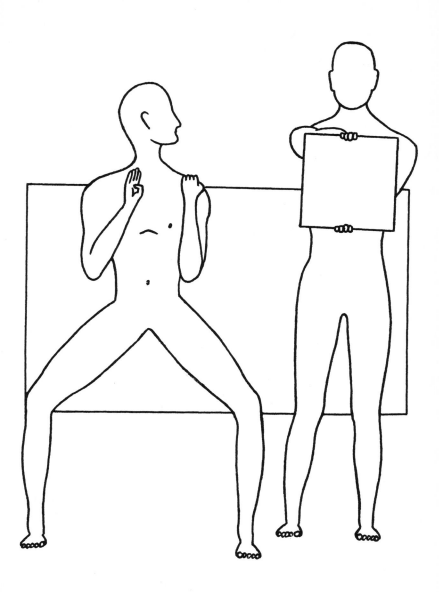

Figure 86

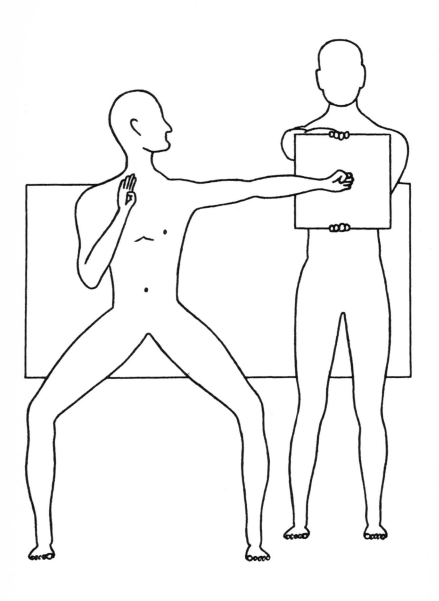

Figure 87

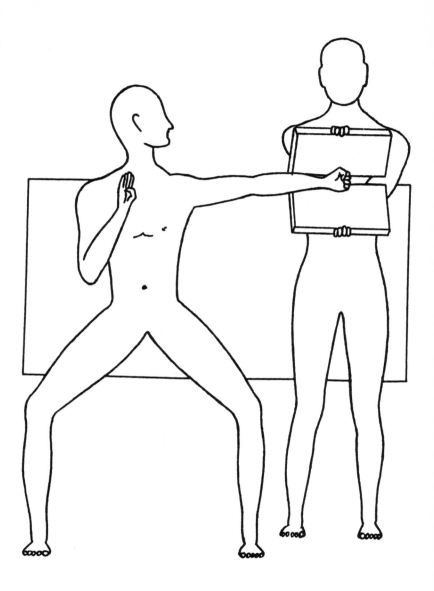

Figure 88

they are in the other three hand strikes. It is, however, an invaluable weapon in combat and should not be discounted. Again, keep the four elements in mind while preparing yourself for the attempt.

SUTO

As noted earlier in the text, the suto will develop much more quickly than the other hand weapons. If you are breaking two boards with a straight punch, it is likely that you will be capable of breaking two cement slabs, as illustrated in Figures 89, 90, and 91, with your suto.

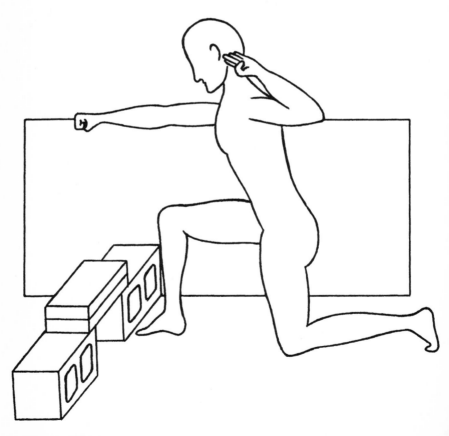

Figure 89

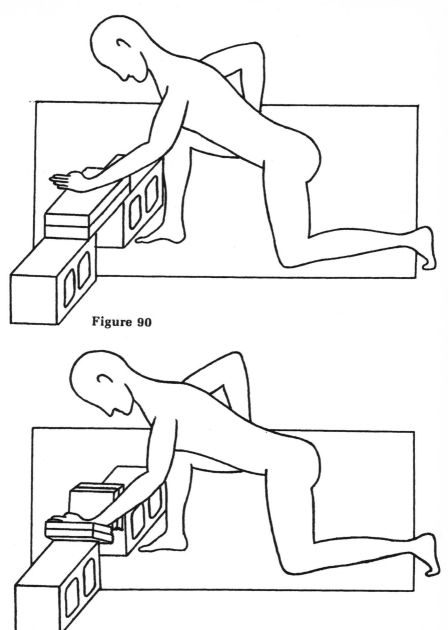

Figure 90

Figure 91

When we began training the suto, we discussed the location of the full chamber position for the suto. Figure 89 depicts that position. Because it is not safe to hold cement slabs for breaking, they are pictured here supported at each end by a standard cement block. A one-inch overlap onto the supporting blocks is sufficient.

Observing Figures 89, 90, and 91, notice first that the opposing hand begins extended outward and is chambered to the punching position on impact of the suto. Also note that the position of the body is different in all three illustrations. When cement blocks or bricks are being broken, the body weight should be used to maximize the power of the stroke. As these three illustrations demonstrate, the upper body should follow the stroke.

PALM STRIKE

The palm strike has no specific chamber position. It can be held in the form in which the suto is held, or it can be positioned as in Figure 92. Note here the positions of the upper body in Figures 93 and 94 as the movement progresses to the final break. Like the suto, the palm power will be increased by bringing the body weight with the strike. As discussed in the punch instructions, keep the four elements in mind.

Like the suto, the palm strike's power source utilizes centrifugal force as well as muscle and the technical structure of the movement. The potential for power is therefore very great. Your initial breaking attempts with the palm are likely to be successful if your hand is properly conditioned, but remember where you started in the conditioning process. Do not start with a hard breaking attempt. You can always make a second and third attempt according to how the first break affected your hand.

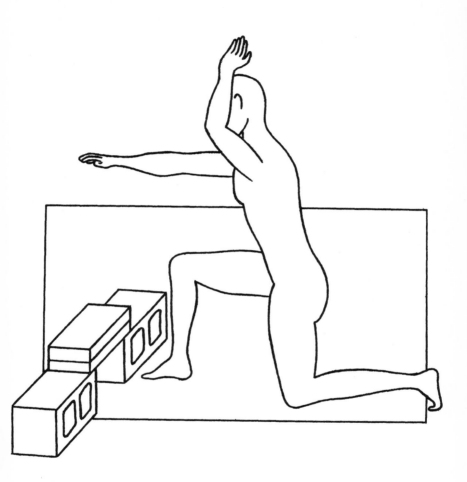

Figure 92

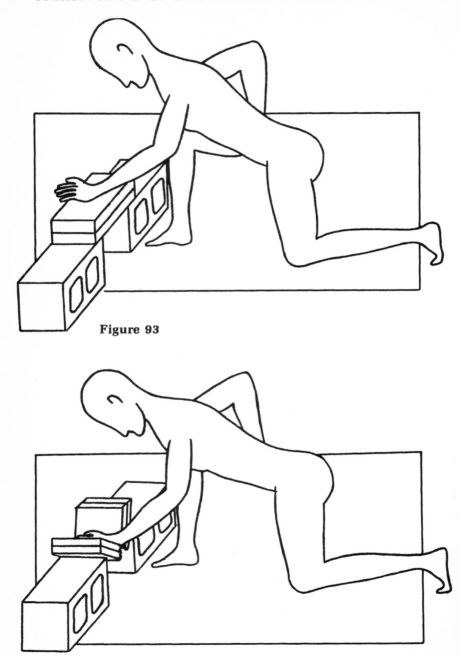

Figure 93

Figure 94

FRONT KICK

When we began training the breaking weapons, hands were worked one day, feet the next. Do not alter the sequence now. When you have fifteen or twenty breaking sessions under your belt, you will have enough experience and enough of an understanding of your body's capabilities and limitations to combine hand and foot breaking into one day. At this point, you will need all of your mental powers to maintain proper form to reduce the chances of injury. Set up a separate day for breaking with kicks.

Figures 95, 96, and 97 illustrate the sequence of breaking with the front kick. If you have trained according to the instructions given thus far, the form and technique are familiar to you here as they have been in all the breaking instructions in this chapter. The only difference is the increased penetration. Kicks should penetrate from two to twelve inches through a target, according to the width of the object itself. Looking at Figure 96, note that at contact with the boards, the kick is not locked into the open position. The

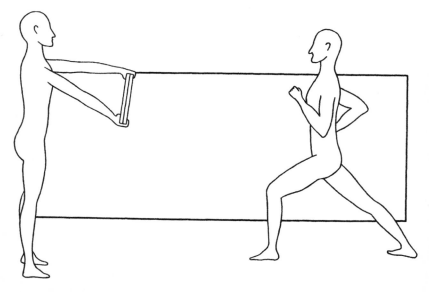

Figure 95

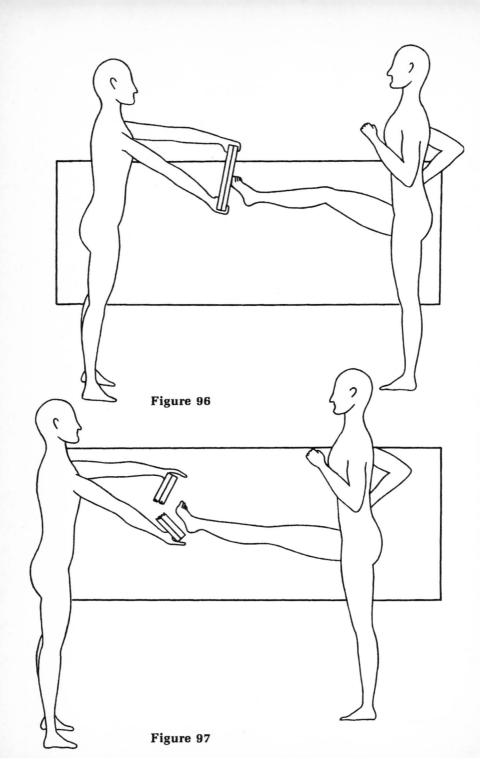

Figure 96

Figure 97

key is to lock *through* the target as depicted in Figure 97. Penetration is critical. All of the instructions discussed in the section on breaking with the hand apply here as well.

HOOK KICK

Your constant training for the hook kick will be seen in your breaking attempt. Balance will be a factor. You should have learned something very important from your breaking attempts with the hands. When you are training on a block, the positive impact force does not affect your balance. When you pass through a breaking object, however, that force may very well carry you forward and off balance if you overpower the object by a great percentage. For hand techniques, that

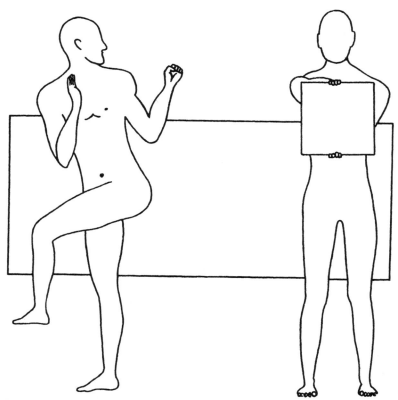

Figure 98

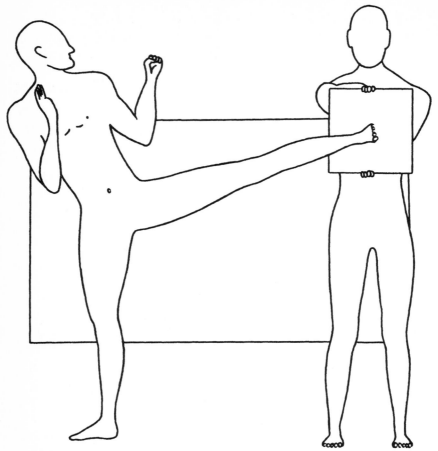

Figure 99

usually means nothing more than a slight loss of upper body balance and a resulting lift of the rear heel of the stance. For the hook kick, that may mean stumbling across the floor or losing your footing altogether and falling. Control is important. Channel your power through the leg and into the foot, and do not allow your body weight to be carried by your kick. Figures 98, 99, and 100 demonstrate the breaking sequence. This form should be exactly the same as your training form. Make several successful breaks with this form before improvising and trying to break with the hook kick out of a different stance or with an advancing movement.

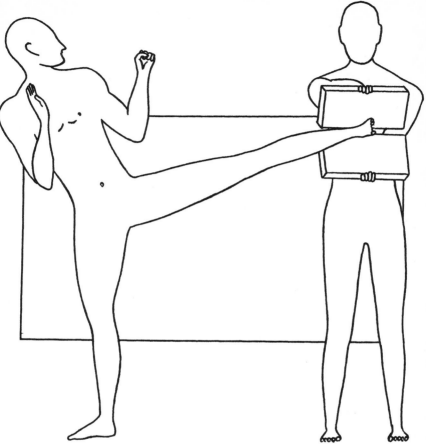

Figure 100

SIDE KICK

In Figures 101 through 103, the side kick is demonstrated in a breaking sequence. Again, your experience on the training block is going to bring you to a successful break. Like the hook kick, the side kick requires balance, but this is the only breaking technique discussed in this text that when unsuccessful will knock you off balance 90 percent of the time. Look at Figure 103. Picture the kick completely extended but the boards not broken. The power has to go somewhere, and there are two confined points of proximity. There will not be enough room to extend the kick if the boards do

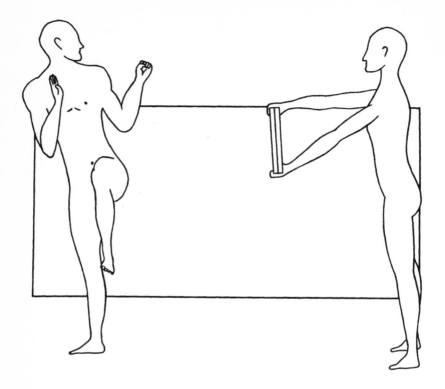

Figure 101

not break. Therefore, when the leg locks into the open position either the person holding the boards will be knocked backward or the person throwing the kick will be forced backward.

I recall attempting a break on eight one-inch boards with a crossing advance side kick out of a straddle stance. When I hit the boards, my kick locked out completely but the boards did not break on the first attempt. The boards were fastened to a wall-mounted breaking rack. The boards did not break, the cement block wall did not move, and the rack was made of angle iron and did not give. My final step with the supporting leg confined my body to a proximity to the target that demanded six inches of penetration through the boards with my foot. When I locked out my leg, there was no room between my stance and the boards for the leg to open fully. As a result, I was shot backward two-thirds of the way across a twenty-four foot mat before I realized it. Be it one board or a hundred boards, if you do not pass through the target and the supporting structure of the target does not give, you will be forced backward. Expect this reaction.

The breaking sequences are all illustrated; you have the technical understanding necessary to develop your weapons. Your efforts and dedication are all that are required beyond this point.

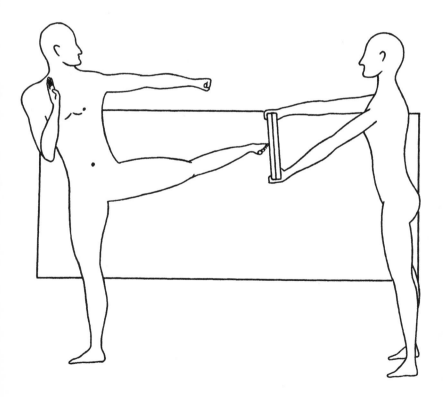

Figure 102

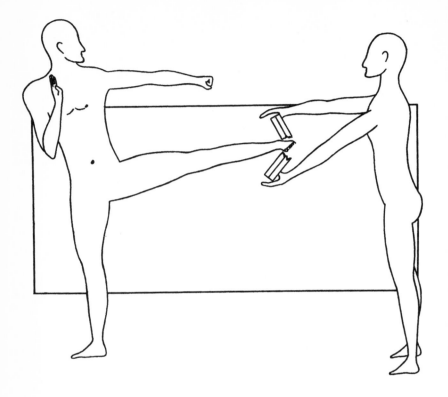

Figure 103

ALAN MITCHEL

PROFILES OF FLIGHT
NORTH AMERICAN P-51
MUSTANG

PROFILES OF FLIGHT

NORTH AMERICAN P-51
MUSTANG
Long-range Fighter

DAVE WINDLE & MARTIN BOWMAN

Pen & Sword
AVIATION

First published in Great Britain in 2011 by
PEN & SWORD AVIATION
An imprint of
Pen & Sword Books Ltd
47 Church Street
Barnsley
South Yorkshire
S70 2AS

ISBN 978 1 84884 581 7

A CIP catalogue record for this book is
available from the British Library

Printed and bound in India
by Replika Press Pvt. Ltd.

Pen & Sword Books Ltd incorporates the Imprints of
Pen & Sword Aviation, Pen & Sword Family History, Pen & Sword Maritime,
Pen & Sword Military, Wharncliffe Local History, Pen & Sword Select,
Pen & Sword Military Classics, Leo Cooper, Remember When,
Seaforth Publishing and Frontline Publishing

For a complete list of Pen & Sword titles please contact
PEN & SWORD BOOKS LIMITED
47 Church Street, Barnsley, South Yorkshire, S70 2AS, England
E-mail: enquiries@pen-and-sword.co.uk
Website: www.pen-and-sword.co.uk

NORTH AMERICAN P-51 MUSTANG

The Mustang story begins in April 1940 when British Direct Purchasing Commission officials visiting America sought a new long-range fighter to supplement the Spitfire and Hurricane. A number of US aircraft manufacturers were called to a conference in New York on 5 April and the delegates included James H 'Dutch' Kindelberger, president of North American Aviation Incorporated, who was accompanied by the company's executive vice-president, J. Leland Attwood. When Curtiss-Wright Corporation offered to supply the Curtiss H-87 (P-40D), which was already in production, it was suggested that North American could ease the supply problem by assisting in production of the aircraft. Then Kindelberger offered to design and build a new and infinitely superior fighter specifically developed to meet the British requirement using the same 1,150-hp Allison V-1710-39 engine. The British Purchasing Commission accepted their proposal but the contract also called for various types of other fittings and armament to be provided by the British, who specified that the cost of each aircraft should not exceed $40,000. North American's only previous experience in fighter design and construction was limited to the NA-50A, which had been designed in 1939 for Siam (now Thailand). However, Kindelberger had studied accounts of air combat in Europe and he had already conceived the broad outlines of a new combat-worthy fighter, designated NA-73. Also, much useful technical data was obtained from the Curtiss-Wright Corporation. The first prototype was not built from production drawings, but rather from design layouts so that a faster rate could be achieved. All told, 3,500 original drawings were required, in addition to a wind-tunnel test programme and a structural test programme, which had to be virtually completed prior to the first flight. The design and production team worked sixteen hours each day, six days a week, finishing at 1800 hours.

Mustang Is of 168 Squadron RAF at Odiham in 1942. **(via Harry Holmes)**

Kindelberger and Attwood called a meeting of the design team at North American, including: Raymond H. Rice (chief engineer); chief design engineer, German-born Edgar Schmued, who had previously worked for Fokker and Messerschmitt; E. J. Horkey (aerodynamicist); and Ken Bowen (project engineer). Arthur G. Patch and John F. Steppe were to oversee wing and fuselage design respectively. Rice ordered a low-drag, high-lift wing, while Horkey submitted what were then considered radical ideas for an aerofoil section. Rice and Schmued planned the NA-73 for mass production with a low, square-cut wing, whose laminar-flow aerofoil had its maximum thickness well aft, similar to aerofoils introduced by the National Advisory Committee for Aeronautics (NACA), giving it the lowest drag of any fighter yet built. A radiator scoop was streamlined into the underside of the fuselage underside behind the pilot, while keeping the fuselage cross-section to the smallest depth possible. The low-drag wing was perfect for high-speed flights over long distances but it meant the aircraft would have a high landing speed so flap design was of vital importance. North American engineers were worried that all of these advanced features would cause long delays when the aircraft went into production but, in the event, their fears proved groundless. Even before the first flight took place, design for production had already started and Ken Bowen was given the job of chief production project engineer.

An Australian pilot, Flying Officer D. W. Samson, with his very early Mustang I (AG431), one of the first to arrive in Britain for the RAF. (IWM)

The NA-73X prototype was assembled in an astonishing 78,000 engineering hours, 127 days, although the 1,100-hp Allison V-1710-39 (F3R) engine was not yet installed and the wheels were borrowed from an AT-6 basic trainer. After several modifications the NA-73X was flown for the first time on 26 October 1940 from Mines Field (now Los Angeles International Airport) in the hands of project test pilot Vance Breese. The prototype showed excellent handling characteristics and early test flights proved to be a great success; the NA-73X soon achieved 382mph at 14,000ft,

North American P-51 Mustang

Mustang IIIs of 19 Squadron RAF. (IWM)

Britain by the US Government, on condition that two of the initial batch were transferred to the Army Air Corps for testing. The fourth and tenth aircraft were allotted the designation XP-51 and the first was flown to Wright Field, Ohio, on 24 August, while the second aircraft (AG346) was accepted by RAF representatives in September. It began a long journey by American cargo ship through the Panama Canal to England and was unloaded at Liverpool docks on 24 October 1941. On 29 May 1941, 320 NA-73s were ordered. A further order was placed for 300 slightly improved NA-82 aircraft, the order being completed in July 1942. At least twenty Mustang Is were lost at sea and another ten were diverted to the Soviet Union before the end of 1941 and were used against Finland.

A Lend-Lease contract approved on 25 September 1941 added 150 NA-91s to the production schedule. These differed from the initial production aircraft by having self-sealing fuel tanks and four 20mm cannon replacing the armament of eight machine guns. A clause in the contract allowed the US government to claim the aircraft in a national emergency and

equal to the British Spitfire. However, during the fifth flight on 20 November 1940 the NA-73X ran out of fuel after a fuel switching error. The pilot attempted a wheels-down landing on farmland and the prototype flipped over onto its back after entering a newly ploughed field. The aircraft was deemed to be a write-off but the British Direct Purchasing Commission had been more than satisfied and production was assured. The first Mustang I was flown on 23 April 1941 and was then retained by the company for necessary testing. The first production model for the RAF (AG345) flew on 1 May 1941. On 4 May the Mustang was cleared for sale to

A P-51B is tested before the test flight at the Lockheed Reassembly plant at Liverpool on 14 December 1943. (USAF)

only ninety-three NA-91s were supplied to the RAF, designating the variant as the Mustang IA. Fifty-five were diverted to the USAAC as the P-51-1NA and were later converted to photographic reconnaissance aircraft with the designation P-51-2-NA (later F-6A) with two cameras behind the cockpit for tactical reconnaissance duties. They were sent to the 68th Observation Group, whose 154th Squadron flew the first USAAF photo reconnaissance mission on 9 April 1943. (In 1943 thirty-three P-51A-10s were converted to F-6B standard and they were first sortied across the English Channel by the 107th TRS on 20 December 1943.) The remaining two aircraft were diverted to the XP-78 project in the USA after testing by the USAAF of its XP-51 prototypes had confirmed RAF findings of their deficiency in high-altitude performance, a weakness explored in the UK by the experimental installation of Rolls-Royce Merlin 61 and 65 engines.

RAF test pilots at the Aeroplane and Armament Experimental Establishment (A&AEE) at Boscombe Down, Wiltshire, and the Air Fighting Development Unit (AFDU) at Duxford, Cambridgeshire, had soon proved that the Mustang was superior to the Kittyhawk, Airacobra and Spitfire V in both speed and manoeuvrability at low altitudes. Top speed went from 328mph at 1,000ft to 382mph at 13,000ft. Equipment included armour, leak-proof tanks, two .50-calibre guns with 400rpg placed low in the nose and two more in the wings inboard of four .30-calibre guns with 500rpg. When it became apparent that performance declined significantly over 15,000ft due to the lack of any supercharging on the Allison power plant, it was decided to operate the Mustang in the armed tactical reconnaissance role with an oblique camera fitted behind the pilot instead of using it as an interceptor. Even so, a speed of almost 353mph at 8,000ft made the Mustang ideal for ground attack and tactical reconnaissance. The type replaced the Curtiss Tomahawk in eleven UK-based Army Co-operation squadrons and provided the equipment of twelve others. The first Mustang IAs began equipping 2 RAF Army Co-operation Squadron at Sawbridgeworth in April 1942 and made their operational debut on 5 May 1942 when a Mustang I of 26 Squadron at Gatwick flew a 1-hour 40-minute tactical reconnaissance sortie of part of the French coast, during which hangars at Berk airfield and a train near La Fesnesie were strafed. By May, six squadrons were working up on the new fighter. The Mustang I's first operational sortie was on 27 July. On 19 August photo reconnaissance Mustangs of Nos 26 and 239 Squadrons, and Nos 400 and 414 RCAF, flew a total of 72 sorties throughout the day, photographing German defence dispositions around the French port of Dieppe prior to the costly commando raid. Nine Mustangs were shot down by flak and FW 190s and several more damaged; two of them beyond repair. Flying Officer H. H. Hill, an American volunteer from Pasadena, California, of 414 Squadron became the first Mustang pilot to score a victory in combat. Cross-Channel sweeps and low-level sorties over enemy-held territory were highly successful and in October the Allison-powered Mustang became the first RAF single-engined single-seat fighter to penetrate German airspace from England when the type attacked the Dortmund-Ems Canal. Mustangs flew defensive patrols along the south-west coast of England and escorted maritime reconnaissance aircraft on operations in the Bay of Biscay. Following the disbandment of Army Co-operation Command in June 1943, the Mustang squadrons temporarily joined RAF Fighter Command before being absorbed into the new 2nd Tactical Air Force (TAF). Fifteen squadrons served the RAF in January 1943, with five remaining in June 1944 and two serving in the low-altitude role until the war's end.

In the autumn of 1942 Lieutenant Colonel Thomas Hitchcock (later killed while flying a Mustang), the US military attaché in London, encouraged by the Ambassador, J. G. Winant, suggested to Washington that the Mustang be developed as a long-range fighter fitted with the Rolls-Royce Merlin engine. Hitchcock reported that the P-51 was one of the best, if not *the* best fighter airframes developed and

P-51B 43-12151 Peggy *in the 355th Fighter Squadron, 354th Fighter Group, at Boxted, Essex.* (USAF)

advised its development as a high-altitude fighter by mating it with the Merlin 61 engine, with its two-stage, two-speed supercharger rather than the single-stage, two-speed of the XX, and which produced a top speed of 400mph at 30,000ft. (An early concept, tried in mock-up form, was to position the engine behind the pilot with an extension shaft driving the propeller, rather like the Allison-powered Bell P-39 Airacobra. This idea, however, was rejected and the Merlin mounted in the conventional position in the nose with the intercooler radiator beneath it.) Eddie Rickenbacker endorsed this opinion and Air Marshal Sir Trafford Leigh-Mallory had four Mustang Is delivered to Rolls-Royce at Hucknall, near Derby, for conversion to Mustang Xs, with the first in the air by 13 October 1942. Data on this work was sent to the United States and North American was issued a contract on 31 July 1942 for two XP-78 aircraft (changed in September 1942 to XP-51B (NA-101)) to be converted from Lend-Lease P-51s, equipped with the Packard Motor Company of Detroit licence-built V-1650-3 Merlin and two-stage supercharger, rated by the Air Force at 1,295hp at 28,750ft, with 1,595 war-emergency hp available to 17,000ft. The first US Packard Merlin Mustang flew on 30 November 1942, with a four-bladed Hamilton propeller for better high-altitude performance compared with the three-bladed propellers of the earlier models and the up-draught carburettor intake positioned below, instead of above, the engine. The intercooler was incorporated in a redesigned main radiator assembly in the existing ventral position amidships and new ailerons were fitted. The XP-51B aircraft demonstrated a maximum speed of 441mph at 29,800ft and the XP-51B configuration was selected to replace the P-51A.

The RAF's adoption of the Mustang for use in a ground-attack role had led in the spring of 1942 to the USAAF's procurement of 500 A-36A aircraft; named Apache initially but later the British name Mustang was adopted. These were delivered from October 1942 to March 1943. They differed from the P-51 in having the 1,325hp Allison V-1710-87 engine (which was boosted for low-altitude operations), wing-mounted lattice-type air-brakes, underwing bomb racks for two 500lb bombs and six .50-calibre gun armament

A P-51B Mustang in the 354th Fighter Group at Boxted, Essex in 1943. (USAF)

Major James H. Howard, 356th Squadron CO, 354th Fighter Group, who was awarded the Medal of Honor for his actions on 11 January 1944 when he battled with more than thirty German fighters that were attacking B-17s of the 401st Bomb Group near Oschersleben. His brave, single-handed action undoubtedly saved the formation. **(USAF)**

(including two in the nose). The air-brakes proved unsatisfactory and were eventually wired shut. Three groups, formerly using the Vengeance two-seaters, went into combat with the single-seat North American A-36A. These were actually P-51 Mustang fighters begun on 16 April 1942 that had been completed as dive bombers. Combat missions

against Sicily, Pantelleria and Lampedusa were started from Tunisia on 6 June 1943 by the 27th Fighter Group (re-designated the 27th Fighter-Bomber Group in August), joined by the A-36As of the 86th Bombardment Group (Dive) (soon named 86th FBG) in July. Both Groups were among the aircraft that supported *Husky* (the codename for the seaborne invasion of Sicily) landings on Sicily before taking part in the Italian campaign that followed. Despite some heavy losses the A-36As wrought tremendous havoc. Every conceivable type of target was attacked, from troops and vehicles of the Hermann Goering Division to flak batteries and railway marshalling yards. An American war correspondent, reporting on the A-36A, cabled:

> The scream of this plane when it dives would shake any man. It makes a Stuka sound like an alley cat. When it levels off at the bottom and lands those bombs right on target, it zooms away as a heavily-gunned fighter, looking for Axis troops to strafe, for enemy planes or tanks or trains to destroy. It's a hot ship ... plenty fast and plenty rugged. No wonder our jubilant pilots nicknamed it 'Invader'.

On 10 September 1943 the 27th FBG prevented three German *panzer* divisions from reaching the Salerno beachhead; this earned the group a Distinguished Unit Citation. Another outstanding feat by the A-36A was the sinking by two aircraft that same month of a 50,000-ton

P-51B WR-P 42-106950 in the 354th Fighter Squadron, 355th Fighter Group. (USAF)

Italian transport vessel of the Conti Di Savoia class while it was riding at anchor at Baguara. The A-36As flew 23,373 sorties and dropped over 16,000 bombs before being replaced by P-47s in 1944.

In India the A-36A was operated by the 311th Fighter-Bomber Group. It was the only liquid-cooled attack aircraft and the last dive bomber to be used in the war by the USAAF. Its success demonstrated the value of single-seat fighter-bombers and led to widespread use of later P-51 and P-47 models on close-support missions. One A-36A example was sent to the UK and evaluated by the RAF, though no production order was placed. Almost simultaneously with the procurement of the A-36As, the USAAF ordered 1,200 (NA-99) P-51A fighters. With North American Aviation planning a build rate of 20 per day, 310 were delivered from March to May 1943. These were powered by the 1,200hp V-1710-81 with war-emergency boost and armed with four .50-calibre wing guns with 1,260 rounds and wing racks for two 500lb bombs or drop tanks. The first P-51A group was the 54th, which remained in Florida for replacement training, while later P-51As went to Asia to the 23rd, 311th and 1st Air Commando groups and flew their first missions on Thanksgiving Day 1943. Fifty P-51As were allocated to the RAF, which designated them Mustang II, and thirty-five were converted as tactical reconnaissance F-6B aircraft for the USAAF.

The first P-51B-1-NA powered by the Packard-built V-1650-3 Merlin was flown on 5 May 1943. North American's Inglewood, California, factory built 1,788 P-51Bs (NA-102

Lieutenant Howard A. Spaulding of Monticella, NY, examines the damage to his P-51 upon returning from a strafing mission over Chartres, France. While shooting up an enemy train, he was flying low enough for part of a tree to penetrate the leading edge of his Mustang's wing. **(USAF)**

and NA-104). The P-51B differed from the earlier versions by having a strengthened fuselage and redesigned ailerons. When another fuel tank was added behind the cockpit, and with its two 108- or 150-gallon drop tanks below the wings, the Mustang had the range needed to accompany bombers to any target in Germany. Armament was still four .50-calibre guns – half that of a P-47 – and gun stoppages due to a combination of factors were commonplace. The laminar wing section was too thin to accommodate the .50-calibre machine guns in the normal upright position so they were canted over about 30 degrees. Thus, the ammunition feed trays had to curve upward slightly and then down again to enable link-belted rounds to enter the gun at the right angle. Gun jams were almost inevitable if they were fired when the pilot was pulling about four g. Worse still, all four guns could stop firing altogether. Robert J. Goebel, a P-51B/D pilot who scored eleven victories in 1944, wrote.

On the Mustang, there was no way to cycle the guns from the cockpit; if one or more of the guns jammed in flight, you were out of luck until you landed. I guess I am one of those people who learn by doing. Well, I did and I learned. On one of the next missions, I got into a wild melee and was taking all manner of ridiculous shots. Suddenly all four guns stopped firing. My heart stopped beating a split second later. Talk about a tiger turning into a rabbit! I was stunned, and for an instant I could think of nothing better to do than follow my quarry through his aerial gymnastics, with only the GSAP camera going. I figured that I better let go before he got wise to my problem and gave me an even bigger one. He made a sham turn to the right and I went left, diving away at full throttle. Nothing quiets the nerves like putting a little distance between you and the nearest enemy fighter, especially when you are impotent.

The last 350 P-51B-15-NAs were powered by the V-1650-7 (Merlin 68), which had a war emergency rating of 1,695hp at 10,300ft and produced a maximum speed of 439mph at 25,000ft. In August 1943 a new factory at Dallas, Texas, began deliveries of 350 P-51C-1-NT Mustangs with the V-1650-3, followed by 1,400 P-51Cs powered by the V-1650-7. The P-51C had increased internal fuel capacity and a British-designed Malcolm bulged, frameless sliding hood similar to the Spitfire canopy as a temporary measure to improve the rearward view. R. Malcolm's design was fitted to most RAF Mustang IIIs, as well as to a number of USAAF P-51Bs and Cs and F-6s. By 1944 a major re-design began to fit a streamlined 'bubble' canopy on a cut-down rear fuselage. In 1943 71 Merlin-powered P-51B-ls and 20 P-51C-ls received by the USAAF were modified as F-6C tactical reconnaissance aircraft while 136 F-6Ds and 163 F-6Ks were built at Dallas beginning in November 1944. All of these aircraft still carried their wing guns and frequently used them; the last German fighter destroyed in the war was an FW 190, downed by an F-6C on 8 May 1945.

After the war General 'Hap' Arnold frankly admitted that it had been 'the USAAF's own fault' that the Mustang had not been employed operationally very much earlier. Inexplicably, USAAF planners had considered the Mustang more suitable as a tactical aircraft than as a long-range escort fighter and in November 1943 the first deliveries of P-51Bs to England were to the tactical Ninth Air Force at the expense of 8th Fighter Command. General Ira Eaker, commanding 8th Bomber Command, knew that deep-penetration missions were finished unless a proven long-range escort fighter could be found. 'At this point nothing was more critical than the early arrival of the P-38s and P-51s', he said. The P-51B was not only capable of meeting the Bf 109s and FW 190s on even or better terms; it could escort the B-24s and B-17s to their targets and back again. The first P-51B group there, the 354th Fighter Group, flew its first cross-Channel sweep on 1 December 1943. It was not until the 357th Fighter Group and its P-51Bs were transferred to the Eighth Air Force in exchange for a P-47-equipped Fighter Group that the Eighth had its long-range escort fighter. The first P-51 escort mission

P-51s at Filton near Bristol on 18 April 1944. (USAF)

P-51D 44-14507 *Tangerine* in the 364th Fighter Squadron, 357th Fighter Group, landing at Leiston in the summer of 1944. *(USAF)*

for the bombers was finally flown on 5 December. By 8 December the 354th, the 357th and the 362nd, which flew P-47s, had been placed under 70th Fighter Wing control in IX Fighter Command, but the 354th came under the control of 8th Fighter Command and provided long-range escort for Eighth Air Force B-17s and B-24s. On 11 December, using drop tanks, the Mustangs ranged as far as Emden to support B-17s bombing the German port. Two days later, when in a record flight, 649 bombers bombed naval targets at Bremen, Hamburg and Kiel, the 354th flew to the limit of its operational radius with the smaller tanks of 480 miles to cover the B-17s. Lieutenant Colonel Don Blakeslee, CO of the 4th Fighter Group, who was assigned to the 354th Fighter Group to help them enter combat, was so impressed with the P-51B that when he returned to Debden he argued forcefully for his group to be equipped with the Mustang, which they were at the end of February 1944. Blakeslee's total victory score was 14.5, seven of which were scored flying P-51B/D aircraft.

As Air Vice Marshal 'Johnnie' Johnson, the top scoring RAF fighter pilot in the Second World War, once said, 'The Mustangs had seven league boots. They imposed a severe problem on the enemy's defence system and added tremendous impetus to the daylight offensive.' The Mustang's range of 2,080 miles was far in excess of that available in other fighters of the day and this was achieved by the internal

fuel it carried. A total of 92 gallons were contained in each wing and this was supplemented by two 75-gallon under-wing drop tanks and a fuselage tank, an 85-gallon design afterthought, behind the cockpit. When this tank was anything more than two-thirds full the Mustang had a potentially vicious handling peculiarity that meant that pilots

P-51B 42-106819 6N-B *Mary Queen of Scotts flown by Major Donald A. 'Don' Larson in the 505th Fighter Squadron, 339th Fighter Group. (USAF)*

could not perform even modest combat manoeuvres and a Bf 109, even in the hands of an average pilot, could easily out manoeuvre a Mustang that had a full fuselage tank. The result, owing to an aft-loaded centre of gravity, would usually end with the pilot losing control, pitching over and entering a fatal spin. Consequently, once airborne, pilots bled off some fuel from the fuselage tank before they began to use fuel from the drop tanks. Theoretically, pilots would be well inside Germany before they exhausted their external fuel load and the longer they could retain their tanks the better. Robert J. Goebel recalls:

With the full 85 gallons of fuel in the fuselage tank, the aft centre of gravity in a maximum-rate turn caused a stick reversal; the plane tended to wrap the turn tighter without any back pressure on the stick. In short, the plane behaved like a pregnant sow. The standard procedure was to burn the fuselage tank down to about 30 gallons immediately after take-off even before going on the external tanks. That way, if the external tanks had to be jettisoned unexpectedly, you were already in a condition from which you could fight…. The fuel-tank selector, which had five positions corresponding to the five tanks, controlled fuel flow. The selector was in the centre, below the instrument panel, just forward of the stick. Pilots would take off using fuel from the left side 75 gallon wing tank and once airborne and in formation, switch to the fuselage tank situated aft of the cockpit… If the fuel selector was on one of the external positions when the tanks were dropped, the engine didn't run very well when it started sucking air. No permanent harm was done, but the momentary silence in the cockpit invariably rattled an already wrought-up new guy. If the truth be known, it rattled some old guys, too.

I felt comfortable in the P-51 Mustang. It was like a favourite warm jacket or an old pair of shoes; everything was friendly and familiar, the feel, the look, even the smell. With my eyes closed I could see every gauge and dial, find every switch and lever merely by reaching out and putting my hand to it…The engine instruments were pretty much the same as those for all liquid-cooled engines, even the old P-40s at Moore Field: manifold pressure and tachometer, fuel and oil pressure, oil and coolant temperature and hydraulic pressure. Ditto the flight instruments. Although the turn and bank and the artificial horizon were frequently used going through overcast, the compass and directional gyro, the altimeter and clock were the key gauges now… The large amounts of fuel the Mustang carried eased many of the worries about navigation. An awful lot of navigation errors could be rectified by the simple expedient of changing course, hunting around a bit, or even backtracking, if necessary.

P-51D *Tar Heel* in the 505th Fighter Squadron, 339th Fighter Group, at Fowlmere pictured at Bassingbourn. *(USAF)*

Lieutenant Colonel Bill Crump recalls:

The P-51 was the ultimate fighter aircraft and the end of an era. When you shove 61 inches of manifold pressure to that Rolls-Royce Merlin and that enormous four

A P-51 veteran of sixty-three missions in the MTO (Mediterranean Theatre of Operations). (USAF)

bladed propeller starts chewing on the atmosphere up ahead, you receive an undeniable communiqué. You are going somewhere aloft, and fast. Then when you start manoeuvring this creature and become aware of the positively sensual balance of the controls, you just might find yourself humming a love song. Every airman worth his tin wings nurses a sneaking suspicion he is a natural as a fighter pilot and those who have blessed with a Mustang are certain of it.

In the early months of 1944 US Mustangs began operating in Burma in support of airborne troops attacking Japanese lines of communication 200 miles behind the Assam–Burma front. Colonel (later Major General) Charles M. 'Sandy' McCorkle, an ace on both Mustangs and Spitfires in Italy in 1943–44, flew the P-51B in Florida after his unit had been recalled from combat duty with P-39s in the Aleutians. He recalled that the P-51B:

… felt slightly heavier than the A and you could sense the difference in the engines – the Allison slower and lower in pitch, the Packard somewhat more chattery, and permitting higher manifold pressure. But once past 20,000ft, with the high blower in, the B really came alive. It sped upward with an excellent rate of climb, to about an indicated 43,000ft, a new part of the world for most fighter pilots. This was truly the very best fighter that the USAAF had. What an engine! It was still fast, like the P-

A flight of 31st Group Mustangs at San Severo in Italy led by Captain John J. Voll, the Fifteenth Air Force's top ace with twenty-one aircraft destroyed, in his P-51D 44-15459 HL-B American Beauty. HL-C 44-13311 is flown by the 308th Squadron CO, Major Leland P. 'Tommy' Molland, who scored 10.5 victories. (USAF)

51A at low altitudes, and it had even greater range, which we Aleutian pilots could appreciate.

By 1944, fourteen P-47 groups, three P-51 groups and one P-38 fighter group were serving in the Ninth Air Force in England. On 11 January 1944 the Mustang was still a well-kept secret and the 354th Fighter Group was the pioneer Mustang group in the ETO (European Theatre of Operations). Major James H. Howard, an ex-Flying Tigers P-40 pilot in China and now CO of 356th Squadron, displayed 'conspicuous gallantry and intrepidity above and beyond the call of duty in action with the enemy near Oschersleben

P-51D 44-13887 Little Joe in the 363rd Fighter Squadron, 357th Fighter Group, at Leiston with ground crew. (USAF)

when he came to the rescue of some Fortresses'. Howard was flying his usual P-51B, *Ding Hao!* (Chinese for 'very good') when the 354th provided support for a formation of B-17s on a long-range mission deep into enemy territory. As the P-51s met the bombers in the target area numerous rocket-firing Bf 110 *Zerstörer* fighters attacked the bomber force. The 354th engaged and Howard destroyed one of the Bf 110s, but in the fight lost contact with the rest of his group. He immediately

P-51D Jake The Snake *in the 358th Fighter Squadron, 355th Fighter Group. (via D. Crow)*

returned to the level of the bomber formation and saw that the B-17s of the 401st Bomb Group were being heavily attacked by German fighters and that no 'little friends' were on hand. Howard dived into the formation of more than

Lieutenant Bruce W. Rowlett of Long Beach, California, the 357th Fighter Squadron Operations Officer in the 361st Fighter Group, gives the thumbs up to Sergeant William R. Jensen of Provo, Utah. (USAF)

thirty German fighters and for thirty minutes single-handedly pressed home a series of determined attacks. He shot down two more fighters and probably destroyed another and damaged one other. Towards the end of his action, Howard continued to fight with one remaining machine gun and his fuel supply dangerously low. Major Howard's brave, single-handed action undoubtedly saved the formation. He was awarded the Medal of Honor, the only one ever awarded to a fighter pilot flying from England. Howard's total score was 8.333 – all except two victories being scored flying the Mustang, from 20 December 1943 to 8 April 1945.

In February 1944 there was great competition among American fighter pilots to get their hands on the Mustang and Lieutenant Colonel Don Blakeslee, the CO of the 4th Fighter Group, which was equipped with P-47s, pleaded with General Bill Kepner, commanding 8th Fighter Command, to exchange their old Thunderbolts for them. But a great daylight offensive was planned, the Normandy invasion would take place within three months, and so the answer was that they did not see how Blakeslee's group could become non-operational for several weeks while they re-trained on to the new fighter. 'That's OK, General, sir,' replied Blakeslee. 'We can learn to fly them on the way to the target!' Conversion to the P-51 Mustang took place after a P-51B trainer arrived at Debden or the 'Eagle's Nest' as it was known on 22 February and each pilot logged on average about forty

The Army Expansion Act of 1939 brought into existence the all-black 99th Pursuit Squadron in January 1940, which trained at the traditionally Negro Tuskegee Institute in Alabama. After February 1944 the 332nd Fighter Group, commanded by Lieutenant Colonel Benjamin O. Davis Jr, fought in Italy in the 12th Air Force. Flying P-40s and later P-51s, the Group destroyed 108.5 enemy aircraft in the air and another 150 on the ground. On escort missions they never lost or abandoned a bomber. (USAF)

minutes on the new type. Within twenty-four hours Blakeslee was leading twenty-two P-51Bs on a fighter sweep over France.

Not all pilots liked changing from P-47s to P-51s. At Duxford, when the 78th Fighter Group were told that they would be changing from 'the good old P-47s that would stand almost any punishment to P-51Ds, which were an unknown quantity, no one wanted to change' recalls Captain Pete Keillor. Though the Mustang was certainly more manoeuvrable than the much heavier Thunderbolt, most 'Jug' pilots considered that the P-51 was nowhere near as resilient to flak damage as the P-47. The Thunderbolt could always be counted on to get its pilot home and many were reluctant to change. Even German pilots considered the Mustang to be more vulnerable to cannon fire. Larry Nelson thought that it was 'Merry Christmas' when they each got a 'nice new plane'.

We were given a Pilot's Information File (PIF) to read over and be ready to fly the new plane. There was only room for one in the cockpit, so an instructor was out of the question. Being a young pilot, it seemed like a big order. My first take-off must have been something to behold. The PIF said the Mustang was very touchy. It was much lighter and very noisy in the cockpit compared to the Thunderbolt. I over-controlled greatly. It reacted instantly to rudder and stick movement. We had to learn fast because we would be flying close

P-51D *Texas Terror IV* in the 354th Fighter Squadron, 355th Fighter Group. *(USAF)*

formation soon. After a few take-offs and landings, I had my Mustang 'corralled'.

On 10 February 1944 the long-ranging P-51s could accompany the heavies to their targets and back again but they were powerless to prevent German fighters destroying

A P-51 with auxiliary fuel tanks mounted under each wing. In the cockpit is Lieutenant William E. Pitcher of Spokane, Washington, talking to 1st Lieutenant E. E. Hendricks of Long Island, New York, 2nd Lieutenant Edward E. Phillips of Springfield New Jersey is on the right. (USAF)

29 of the 169 Fortresses despatched. Next day the first P-51Bs joined VIII Fighter Command when the 357th Fighter Group at Raydon, Essex, received them. They flew their first escort mission the next day. During 'Big Week' (20–25 February) Eighth and Fifteenth Air Force bombers and 1,000 fighters were dispatched almost daily on the deepest penetrations into Germany thus far. In the first week of March 1944, P-51Bs flew to Berlin and back for the first time. On 4 March, when the mission was recalled because of bad weather, Don Blakeslee led the 4th Fighter Group spearheading the bombers but the P-51 squadrons became separated in clouds over Germany. Nine Mustangs were engaged by 54 to 60 enemy fighters but managed to escape with the loss of one and claims of six enemy aircraft destroyed. On 6 March, 801 P-38s, P-47s and P-51s of 4th, 354th and 357th Fighter Groups escorted 730 B-17s and B-24s to targets in the suburbs of 'Big-B' (Berlin). Eleven fighters, five of them Mustangs, were lost but the P-51s claimed forty-one enemy aircraft destroyed. On 8 March the 4th Fighter Group claimed sixteen enemy aircraft destroyed on another mission to Berlin. During March the 4th Fighter Group claimed no fewer than 156 confirmed air-to-air victories plus 8 probables and 100 were claimed in just 15 days. On 5 April Mustangs took part in the first large-scale USAAF all-fighter sweep, to the Berlin and Munich areas. It involved a round trip of 1,200 miles.

2nd Lieutenant Ralph 'Kid' Hofer in the cockpit of P-51B-15-NA 42-106924 QP-L *Salem Representative*. He scored fifteen victories in the Second World War, all except two of them on the P-51. He was KIA (Killed in Action) on 2 July 1944 while supporting Fifteenth Air Force bombers over the Balkans during an Eighth Air Force 'Shuttle' mission, flying P-51B-7 43-6746 in aerial combat at Mostar, Yugoslavia. Hofer is the only ace known to have been killed in combat with the Luftwaffe (probably a pilot of JG52). (USAF)

James 'Goody' Goodson, recalling an escort mission 31,000ft over Berlin, said:

… the great fleet of B-17 s sailing majestically through the black puffs of flak. Then the massed Me-109s dived down in a head-on attack. I rolled into a dive and led the group down to cut them off. One [appeared] in my sights, still out of range, but closing fast. A quick glance behind, then concentrating on the 109, seeing the black crosses and, as I pressed the button, the yellow flashes along the grey and black fuselage; then an explosion and a wing and pieces of debris floating past. Racking the P-51 round in a tight turn, blacking out for a moment and when vision clears, pulling up into the next wave of 109s coming down, closing on one of our P-51s. 'Yellow four, break hard right!' The 109 follows this but I'm inside and hit twice in the cockpit. Suddenly, there's nothing but a few of our own P-51s around.

These long missions signalled the beginning of the end of *Luftwaffe* air superiority over the *Reich*. Captain Pete Hardiman recalls:

My only complaint was that we did not get P-51s a year sooner. Even Hermann Goering knew he was licked when he saw B-17s escorted by P-51s over Berlin. My first meeting with the P-51 was March 1944. Compared to any fighter I had seen or flown, she was beautiful. I fell in love at first sight. Finally, I knew that North American Aviation had kept their word and given us the best fighter ever designed. The P-51B could be everything a Spitfire could (except climb) and better by far the most honest airplane, no bad flying habits, its only fault was the 'Chicken coop canopy' along with the razorback body behind. It was very hard to keep check on one's 6 o'clock. We rapidly adapted the British 'Malcolm Hood', which worked so well on the Spitfires. The threat of liquid engine cooling vulnerability with the Merlin engines was only true if all coolant was lost immediately, some nursing was quite possible if the oil cooling remained intact, particularly in colder air. I personally nursed mine home from Frankfurt, with a coolant leak, about 600 miles. Going to Berlin and back in a P-51 was not the most comfortable way to spend one's day but doing it in a P-51 overpowered the discomfort. We could not stand or straighten our legs. Long high altitude flying and oxygen saps one's stamina but having the P-51 Mustang to do it in was a life saver. The P-51D answered all of a fighter pilot's dreams, a wonderful flying machine, a view of the world around, a fantastic gun platform and an airplane designed to combat all enemies at any distance from base and with a well trained pilot aboard a match for any and all comers.

By 1945 fourteen P-51 groups and one P-47 group served the Eighth Air Force, while fourteen P-47 groups, three P-51 groups, and one P-38 fighter group served the Ninth Air Force. The top Mustang group was the 357th, with 609 air and 106 ground kills from 11 February 1944 to 25 April 1945. The Mustangs' advantage of greater endurance than the P-47s saw them regularly running up substantial scores as the P-51s saw widespread use as escort fighters on long-penetration raids deep into Germany. The 4th Group, which used Spitfires, P-47s and P-51s (received in February 1944), had 583 air and 469 ground kills. The top-scoring Mustang aces were George Preddy with twenty-five victories, John C. Meyer with twenty-four, and Don Gentile with twenty-three.

The RAF was second only to the USAAF in Mustang operation. Lend-Lease allocations of the P-51B/C versions for the RAF comprised 308 and 636 respectively, all designated Mustang III, but some were repossessed by the USAAF. The first unit to be equipped was 65 Squadron, which received its first Mustang III in December 1943, but the type did not enter service with the RAF until February 1944 when it began equipping 19 Squadron at Ford. The first 250 ordered had the older, hinged cockpit canopy. With a maximum speed of 442mph at 24,500ft it was more than a match for German propeller-driven fighters in 1944 and could operate far over the continent with the aid of drop tanks. From the spring of 1944, the Mustang III served with

Man O'War 44-73144 in the 354th Fighter Squadron, 355th Fighter Group. (via D Crow)

the Desert Air Force, supporting the 8th Army in Italy, and was flown by 112 and 260 Squadrons and 3 Squadron RAAF and 5 Squadron SAAF of 239 Wing in Eastern Italy. The latter changed over to Mustangs from Curtiss P-40 Kittyhawks. On 5 May, soon after the first unit (260 Squadron) had received Mustangs, both types of aircraft from the wing destroyed the

great Pescara Dam by bombing. Not one Mustang was lost on this operation, which was a remarkable feat to be accomplished by single-seat fighters. No. 239 Wing's Mustangs were responsible for evolving the 'cab-rank' tactics that were subsequently used to equally good effect in northern Europe. The Mustangs, sometimes carrying bombs,

Dear Arabella in the 361st Fighter Group peeling away. (USAF)

patrolled – usually in line astern-above the forward troops during an offensive. The Mustangs awaited radio calls from a mobile observation post with the troops for attacks on specific targets previously located by spotter aircraft. On receiving a call, one or more aircraft from the 'cab-rank' would dive upon the target and drop bombs or strafe it with gunfire. Both the ground controllers and the Mustang pilots used the same photographic map with a grid superimposed upon it and 'Rover David' – as the system was code-named – proved an immediate success. Various modifications of the system were tried from time to time as the war continued, but its principle remained unchanged.

Mustang IIIs continued to escort medium and heavy bombers over the continent in 1944. After the Normandy landings in June 1944 some Mustang squadrons in 2nd Tactical Air Force moved to the Continent to act as fighter-bombers. Mustangs operated on everything from offensive sweeps, escorts to Bristol Beaufighters as far afield as Denmark, anti-*Diver* (V-1 flying bomb) patrols (in a three-month period ending 5 September 1944 Mustangs of 12 Group had destroyed 232 Doodlebugs), barge-busting in the River Seine and, from D-Day, giving close air support to Allied troops. Two Mustangs were used by 617 Squadron to mark targets for the heavies of Bomber Command. By September 1944, two Italian-based Mustang III squadrons – 213 and 249 at Biferno and in the Balkan Air Force – were busy operating over Yugoslavia and Greece. It was in Italy and the Balkans that rocket-firing Mustangs were used. Trials of a Mk V rocket projectile installation were made on a Mustang III at the A&AEE at Boscombe Down. As it greatly reduced

375th Fighter Squadron, 361st Fighter Group, P-51B/Ds from Bottisham on 11 July 1944. The Group CO, Colonel Thomas J. J. Christian, is leading in P-51D 44-13410 Lou IV IV/Athlene. *Christian was shot down and killed on 12 August 1944 in this Mustang. The second P-51D in the formation is E2-S 44-13926, being flown by the Group's third-ranking ace, 1st Lieutenant Urban Drew. Alongside Drew is Lieutenant Bruce Rowlett in 44-13568* Sky Bouncer, *while occupying the No.4 slot in P-51B 42-106811* Suzy G *is Captain Francis Glanker. (USAF)*

P-51D 44-13926 being flown by 1st Lieutenant Urban Drew in the 375th Fighter Squadron. E2-S was hastily sprayed with OD (Olive Drab) paint when VIIIth Fighter Command thought it would have to forward deploy fighters to France soon after D-Day. 44-13926 was written-off in a crash on 9 August while being flown by Lieutenant Don Dellinger, who was killed. (USAF)

the aircraft's speed, rocket-firing Mustangs did not find favour for operations in Northern Europe, although they were acceptable in Italy. USAAF Mustangs in various war zones also used rockets, their weapons often being fired from infantry-type bazookas, whereas the RAF Mustangs were launched from rails. All told, Mustang IIIs and Vs equipped eighteen squadrons of the RAF in the UK and 2nd TAF and six squadrons in the Mediterranean. At the end of 1944 Mustangs of the 2nd TAF were withdrawn and rejoined Fighter Command but Mustangs of 11 and 13 Groups continued to escort US Eighth Air Force daylight raids from the UK until the end of the war.

The P-51D, which replaced the B model at Inglewood in March 1944, was to become the most successful variant of Mustang. It was built in greater quantity than any other variant with a total of 7,956 built; 6,502 at Inglewood and 1,454 at Dallas. From this total 136 were modified as tactical reconnaissance F-6D aircraft and 282 were allocated to the RAF, which designated them Mustang IV. The P-51D differed from earlier versions in having a streamlined bubble (teardrop) canopy with a lowered rear decking to give the pilot all-around vision. The new teardrop hood was introduced onto the production line after the completion of the first four aircraft. Later, a small dorsal fin fairing was added to most P-51D examples to compensate for the loss of keel surface on the rear fuselage. Tail warning radar was also added. Armament was increased to six .50 calibre wing guns with 1,880 rounds. Power was provided by the more powerful Packard Merlin V-1650-7 engine driving a Hamilton propeller. This was the fastest of all Mustangs, having a top speed of 487 mph.

Robert J. Goebel recalls:

The D was a considerably improved airplane. It had a bubble canopy instead of the greenhouse-style enclosure, and the bubble allowed a lot better visibility in the air. Instead of the drab brown paint job, the new planes were NMF – natural metal finish. They fairly glowed in the sky. That we didn't need camouflage any longer testified to the way the air war in Europe was going: We were winning big…. Other changes were less visible to the eye but of equal or greater importance to the pilot. The sight had a 100mm fixed reticule instead of the P-51B's optical sight with a 70mm reticule, which was too small for any angle-off shooting. The new sight made deflection shots and range estimation somewhat easier. More important, the wing had been thickened slightly so that the armament now consisted of six .50-calibre machine guns set upright. Upright guns meant no more jam problem, and for good measure, the P-51D provided half again as much firepower…We soon found

P-51D 44-14254 of the 385th Fighter Squadron, 364th Fighter Group, 67th Fighter Wing, at Honington on 24 October 1944. (USAF)

out that the P-51 Mustang was indeed a different breed of airplane. It was fast, for one thing… Physically it was pleasing to the eye and looked fast, even sitting on the ground.

Power was provided by a V-1650 Rolls-Royce Merlin engine built under licence in the States by Packard, the luxury automobile company. The V-1650 could be taken up to 61 inches of manifold pressure at 3,000 RPM for take-off or, if needed in combat, 67 inches for up to five minutes in Emergency Power. Normally aspirated engines tended to run out of power as altitude increased, usually between 15,000 and 20,000ft. The P-51 had a two-stage blower in the induction system that was controlled automatically with a barometric switch. Around 17,000ft, when the throttle had been advanced almost all the way forward just to maintain normal cruise, the blower would kick into high, the manifold pressure would jump up and the climb could be continued to 30,000ft. The P-51 could be taken a lot higher than that but above 30,000ft the power was way down and the controls had to be handled gingerly.

With external tanks giving a total of 489 US gallons of fuel, the P-51D was comparatively light at 11,600lb and had an

Crew chiefs watch as a 361st Fighter Group Mustang comes in to land. (USAF)

absolute range of 2,080 miles – an endurance of 8½ hours. The P-51D was the most widely used Mustang, with 6,502 P-51D-NAs built in California by July 1945. The Texas factory built 1,454 P-51D-NTs concurrently with 1,337 P-51Ks (similar except for an Aeroproducts four-blade, clipped-tip propeller, which was introduced following the reported shortage of the Hamilton-Standard propeller), 136 F-6Ds and 163 F-6K tactical reconnaissance variants and ten TP-51D two-seat trainers with radio equipment re-located and an additional seat, with full dual control, behind the pilot seat. One TP-51D was further modified for use as a high-speed observation post for the Supreme Allied Commander, General Eisenhower, who flew in it to inspect the Normandy beachheads in June 1944. Ten 5-inch rockets, two 500lb bombs, or drop tanks could be carried below the wings. (In 1951 a further fifteen trainers were converted by Temco (Texas Engineering & Manufacturing Company Inc.).

Another unusual P-51D was the 'hooked' example, which in 1944 underwent deck-landing trials aboard the aircraft carrier USS *Shangri-La*. The trials had been requested by the US Navy as early as May 1943 with a view to employing the Mustang as a ship-borne fighter in the Pacific Theatre but progress was slow, largely due to the need to strengthen the airframe to absorb the landing loads of an arrestor-hook deceleration. By the time the trials began, Grumman F6F Hellcats and Vought F4U Corsairs were operating from

Don Helen in the 353rd Fighter Group.

A Ninth Air Force Mustang photo-reconnaissance aircraft warms up in France for a recon mission. (USAF)

carriers in the Pacific and the Mustang carrier fighter was no longer needed. Nevertheless, the trials went ahead and they proved a complete success.

The P-51D first entered service in Europe in 1944 with the USAAF and RAF (as the Mustang IV). It excelled in high-altitude escort and combat, being superior in speed and manoeuvrability to all *Luftwaffe* piston-engined fighters above 20,000ft. A March 1944 report by AFDU or Air Fighting Development Unit (RAF) made brief comparisons between the P-51B-1 and the Focke Wulf 190 powered by the BMW 801D engine. It stated that the latter was almost 50mph slower at all heights, increasing to 70mph above 28,000ft, and it was anticipated that the new DB603-engined Focke Wulf 190 might be slightly faster below 27,000ft but slower above that height. There appeared to be little to choose in the maximum rate of climb. It was anticipated that the Mustang III would have a better maximum climb than the new FW 190. The Mustang was considerably faster at all heights in a zoom climb and the Mustang could always out-dive the FW 190. When it came to the turning circle the report stated that there was not much to choose. The Mustang was slightly better. 'When evading an enemy aircraft with a steep turn, a pilot will always out-turn the attacking aircraft initially because of the difference in speeds. It is therefore still a worthwhile manoeuvre with the Mustang III when attacked.'

When it came to rate of roll, not even a Mustang III approached the FW 190. The report concluded that:

> In the attack, a high speed should be maintained or regained in order to regain height initiative. A Focke Wulf 190 could not evade by diving alone. In defence a steep turn followed by a full throttle dive should increase the range before regaining height and course. Dog fighting is not altogether recommended. Do not attempt to climb away without at least 250mph showing initially.

German pilots considered the Mustang to be more vulnerable to cannon fire. Eighth Air Force pilots were among the first to wear anti-g suits, which inflated automatically around the calves, thighs and lower body during tight turns and when pulling out from a dive, restricting the blood from draining from the head and trunk and thus delaying 'black-out'. The only slight drawback was that the pilots found that they could then take more g than their P-51s, and sometimes after combat Mustangs landed with deformed wings and a number of popped rivets.

Many in the *Wehrmacht* and the *Kriegsmarine* felt betrayed by the lack of German aircraft on D-Day as there was little sign of *Luftwaffe* activity. The German pilots had been caught almost cold. The bombers were protected by no fewer than thirty-six squadrons of Mustangs and Thunderbolts who initially escorted the 'big friends' but would later break off and strafe ground targets.

Major John A. Storch, CO, 364th Fighter Squadron, 357th Fighter Group, relates:

The basic defensive manoeuvre is to turn into the attacking enemy. Often this will automatically turn a defensive situation into an offensive one. If the German turns with you, the P-51 should be on the tail of the average enemy plane in short order. If, as we have found to be more often the case, the German split-esses for the deck, without top cover, you can split-ess after him. He may out dive you on the way down and out manoeuvre you during this dive, but when you level out on the deck you will probably be able to catch him. When attacked

P-51s taxi out in the early morning in Belgium late in 1944. (USAF)

P-51D 44-13704 B7-H Ferocious Frankie in the 361st Fighter Group flown by Lieutenant Colonel Wallace E. Hopkins, his second Mustang named for his wife. Hopkins was flying this aircraft when he shot down two FW 190s on 8 August 1944 to take his final wartime score to four. He was Group Operations Officer and he flew seventy-six combat missions. (USAF)

by superior numbers, if no cloud cover of help is available, about the only thing you can do is to keep turning into his attacks and take such shots as you can get, hoping to even things up. You should, under such circumstances, continue to watch all the time for an opportunity to make a break for home; however, it does not pay to straighten out on a course unless you are very sure you will be out of accurate firing range. My own opinion is that the best way to make the break is a shallow dive with everything full forward. If the enemy starts to overhaul you again and gets within accurate range, about the only thing to do is to turn again and give him a deflection shot at you. When attacked I like to have my wingman stay close enough that he can take a plane off my tail and I can do the same for him. He is of no help, however, if he stays in so tight that we cannot manoeuvre and are practically one target. The preceding and following statements are completely dependent upon circumstances and no hard and fast rules can be set down.

When it came to offensive tactics Major John B England, CO, 362nd Fighter Squadron, 357th Fighter Group, who finished the war with a score of 17.5 victories, opined:

… the most perfect bounce would be made from out of the sun and from 3,000 to 5,000ft above the enemy. A pilot making a bounce should always instinctively have

the advantage in size speed or altitude, since one can be converted to the other. Flights should fly close formation relying on mutual support between flights or for protection. Jerry will think twice before he jumps 18 planes in good formation. This has been proven many times by our experience. The best defensive manoeuvre

P-51D 44-14771 Willit Run? *in the 351st Fighter Squadron, 353rd Fighter Group, with parafrag bombs on 14 November 1944. (USAF)*

for the P-51 against the common enemy fighter plane is just a simple tight turn. I have never seen one of our fighters shot down in a tight turn, but I have seen our fighters shot down while trying to evade Jerry by diving to the deck or pulling some fancy manoeuvres. I say never be on the defensive list; if you are on the defensive, turn it into an offensive situation immediately. Always let the Hun know you're after him from the beginning.

These tactics took time to refine and the success of these tactics was ably demonstrated on several occasions. On 14 January 1945, P-51s of the 357th Fighter Group, commanded by Colonel Irwin H. Dregne at Leiston, Suffolk, shot down 60.5 enemy aircraft. This was a record for any Eighth Air Force fighter group, which still stood by the end of hostilities in Europe. In all, 161 enemy aircraft were destroyed. 1st Lieutenant 'Big John' Kirla was one of two pilots who shot down four enemy fighters. Kirla wrote:

We dropped tanks and engaged the Jerries at about 27,000ft. I picked out a FW 190 and clobbered him all over. I believe I killed the pilot. He dived inverted to the ground and exploded. My second FW 190 was in a dogfight. I started to fire at him from about 400 yards, closing to fifty yards. He began to tumble and I watched him go into the ground. I looked around for another target and saw a Me 109 shooting down a bomber. I went after him, got on his tail and closed to about thirty yards. He went into a very tight barrel-roll going straight down. I fired a short burst then really gave him the works, clobbering him all over. He flipped over on his back and started to burn. Pieces fell off until; finally, just the framework remained. I laughed and commented to myself on the crazy contraptions they were sending up these days. There wasn't enough of the ship left to crash into the ground. Looking around again I observed two Me 109s flying 180° to the bombers and a P-51 chasing them. The P-51 closed in and got the first Jerry but the second one was sliding onto the Mustang's tail. The Mustang was shot down. I was at close enough range by this time to get some revenge. I began firing at about 200 yards and played with him awhile. He was badly scared. I got tired of that and adjusted my K-14 and opened up at about fifty yards. I filled that 109 full of holes. Pieces started to fly off him and he went down like a falling leaf.

Introduced in the spring of 1944, the K-14 gunsight was fairly advanced for its time. It consisted principally of a piece of slanted, clear glass centred above the instrument panel directly in the pilot's line of sight. Onto the glass was projected a centre dot of yellow light, known as a 'pipper', which was surrounded by a circle formed of eight diamond-shaped dots. Once the pilot set the known wingspan of an

P-51D 44-14495 Dallas Doll in the 352nd Fighter Squadron, 353rd Fighter Group, in December 1944. (USAF)

enemy plane using a knob on the sight itself, he then centred the pipper on his target and, using the control knob mounted on the throttle handle, expanded or contracted the diamonds so that they continually bracketed the target. The K-14 automatically calculated the amount of lead needed for the range of the target, and so long as the pilot kept the pipper centred on the enemy aircraft, and enclosed it tightly within the diamonds, he had an excellent chance of scoring hits.

On 19 March 1945 Mustangs flew 606 effective sorties in support of the bombers. Over one hundred enemy fighters, including thirty-six jets in formation (the largest number yet seen in one formation), were encountered. US fighters claimed forty-two enemy fighters (including three jets) destroyed. On 21 March 1945, 78th Fighter Group Mustangs claimed five Me 262 jet fighters destroyed, three of which were caught at low level after taking off from their airfield. One of the two that were shot down in aerial combat fell to 1st Lieutenant John A. Kirk III, who recalls:

We were positioned at 28,000 feet and above and to the right of the bomber stream in the Meiningen area. Thus I was about 8,000ft above the bombers as they neared the target. The first sighting of a Me 262 came when I saw a B-17 being attacked and bursting into flames. The jet broke off and went into a 45° dive straight ahead. I had peeled off and dove just about straight down as I was slightly ahead of him. My wingman followed me. The airspeed indicator rapidly advanced until it was in the red line, which indicated that the plane was flying at about 550mph. That must have been terminal velocity. However, I had no problems handling my aircraft. He was in my K-14 gunsight, but out of range of my six wing guns. As we dove down to about 15,000ft I knew I was not gaining on him, but he was not pulling away either. I decided to lob some bullets at him, although it was forbidden to fire your guns when your speed was in the red line, as vibration would tear the wings off. Having great faith in the strength of the Mustang, I pulled up the nose so that the gunsight was about one radius above the Me 262. One quick burst and a check on the wings showed them to be all right, so another fast burst was fired. My bullets must have hit his right engine, as smoke appeared. He slowed up and I anticipated his next move. I then pulled up from my steep dive, hoping to gain on him when he levelled out. He pulled up from his dive and we closed fast. Soon I was in perfect firing range. The guns were fired in long bursts as soon as he was centred in my gunsight. Strikes appeared all along his fuselage and wing roots. Suddenly the pilot seemed to 'pop out' of the cockpit and flew back very close to me. I could see him very well. To record the kill, I took a camera shot of the plane crashing

P-51D 44-15587 *Stasia II* in the 352nd Fighter Squadron, 353rd Fighter Group, with two 108-gallon jettisonable wing tanks in December 1944. (*USAF*)

in a ball of flame and the German pilot floating down on his parachute.

The Mustang's extreme range made it a natural choice for bomber escort and fighter sweeps in the Pacific. After the capture of Iwo Jima in February 1945, three P-51D/K Fighter Groups began escorting the B-29 Superfortresses in their assault on the Japanese mainland. The first two groups in action were the 15th and 21st Fighter Groups, which after supporting the invasion forces in the area, flew their first mission to Japan on 7 April when they escorted B-29s of 20th Bomber Command attacking the heavily-defended Nakajima aircraft factory near Tokyo. This involved a round-trip of almost 1,500 miles and the Mustangs claimed twenty-one enemy fighters destroyed for the loss of just two fighters, a feat that earned both groups a DUC (Distinguished Unit Citation). Thereafter, the 15th, 21st and the 506th from May onwards, continued to fly offensive sweeps and long-range escort missions to Japanese targets until the end of the war. On 11 January 1945, during a two-plane reconnaissance mission from Leyte to Luzon in the Philippines, an F-6D flown by Captain William A. Shomo of the 82nd Tactical Reconnaissance Squadron, 71st TRG, intercepted a formation of twelve Japanese fighters escorting a Mitsubishi *Betty* bomber. Shomo destroyed six of the fighters while his wingman, 2nd Lieutenant Paul Lipscombe, claimed three fighters. Captain (later Major) Shomo was awarded the Medal of Honor and 2nd Lieutenant Lipscombe the Distinguished Flying Cross. Captain Shomo had been a licensed embalmer before joining the USAAF and named his F-6D *The Flying Undertaker*!

P-51D 44-14706 *Ginny in the 353rd Fighter Group being dug out of the mud after running off the runway at Raydon on 23 January 1945. (USAF)*

Under the Lend-Lease scheme fifty P-51Ds were supplied to China and forty to Netherlands forces in the Pacific theatre, and some USAAF P-51s were supplied to the AVG (American Volunteer Group) in China. Mustang IIIs and IVs (only 282 P-51Ds and about 400 P-51Ks, because of the demand for long-range fighters in the Pacific) equipped sixteen squadrons of the RAF in the UK, and 2nd TAF and six squadrons in the Mediterranean at the war's end. Over 900 Mk IIIs and almost 9,000 Mk IVs entered service with the RAF and some were still serving with Fighter Command as late as November 1946.

In Italy four fighter groups replaced older types with P-51s (the 31st, 52nd, 325th, and 332nd), which joined the Fifteenth Air Force's three P-38 groups for the war's last year in Europe. Merlin-powered Mustangs were used against Japan in 1944 by the 23rd, 51st, and 311th Groups in China, while the Fifth Air Force received P-51Ds in 1945 for the 3rd Commando, 35th, and 348th Groups. Perhaps the most significant Mustang missions in the Pacific were those flown from Iwo Jima by the 15th, 21st, and 506th Groups to support B-29 attacks against Japan.

In his 'Briefing for P-51 Pilot Instructors' in August 1945, Louis S. Wait, Administrative Test Pilot for North American Aviation at Inglewood, California, said, in part:

The new, heavier, more powerful Packard-built Rolls-Royce engine made necessary a heavier radiator for proper cooling and a heavier four-blade wide-chord propeller to utilize the increased engine power at altitude. The P-51B and C airplanes was an overloaded airplane since the combat weight was increased from 8,000lb to slightly over 9,000lb. As later results demonstrated, the decrease in g factor alone was not a serious complication.... However, the increased engine power and four-blade propeller caused a marked decrease in directional stability. Whereas the pilot previously had to use increasing rudder pressure for increasing sideslip or yaw angles, the rudder forces now tended to decrease at yaw angles greater than 100. If the pilot did not apply sufficient opposite rudder, the airplane tended to increase the skid or sideslip all by itself, eventually resulting in an unintentional snap roll or entry into a spin. Several pilots complained that they could no longer obtain their usual evasive action because of the addition of the dorsal fin and change in the rudder boost tab.

Wait added:

With full fuselage tanks and two 110-gallon external tanks, the gross weight of the P-51D was over 11,600lb, nearly 50% more than the design weight of the airplane … The only way to obtain increased strength or any substantial amount of increased stability was to start from scratch and design a new airplane. This has been

P-51D 44-14321 *Esther* in the 504th Fighter Squadron, piloted by Lieutenant Vernon Barto.
The aircraft crashed on take-off on 5 February 1945. (USAF)

P-51K-5-NT 44-11624 SX-M *Donna-Mite in the 352nd Fighter Squadron,
353rd Fighter Group, landing at Raydon in February 1945. (USAF)*

done in the P-51H … actually structurally no longer a P-51 – it is a brand-new airplane [and] designed to develop over 11g ultimate pullout factor at a design gross combat weight of 9,600lb. Further, the arrangement of the airplane has been changed slightly so that it is always stable, regardless of the disposal of fuel or armament load … The P-51H [is] a truly worthy successor to all previous P-5l Series airplanes.

A new, air superiority lightweight fighter design (NA-105) purely for air-to-air combat with no provision for bombing or ground attack was offered in January 1943 and a contract on 20 July called for five prototypes. Using load factors reduced to British standards and only four guns with 1,000 rounds, and replacing certain non-load-bearing metal components with lightweight plastic components achieved the weight saving and a newly designed wing incorporated many drag-reducing features. The forward 'cranking' of the wing-root leading-edge, which had characterized all previous Mustangs, was eliminated thanks to the use of a simplified undercarriage with smaller wheels To reduce drag further, a larger 'tear-drop' cockpit canopy was fitted, together with a modified radiator fairing, the oil cooler being dispensed with in favour of a heat exchanger attached to the front of the oil tank and employing after-cooler fluid to dissipate the heat in the oil. The long vulnerable oil lines to the rear cooler were thus eliminated and the weight of the system reduced. More

weight saving was achieved by the use of a three-bladed Aeroproducts propeller with hollow steel blades.

The first NA-105, an XP-51F with Packard V-1650-3 (later V-1650-7), flew on 14 February 1944 while the fourth, an XP-51G, flew on 9 August equipped with an imported Rolls-Royce Merlin 145 and a unique five-bladed propeller. The third XP-51F was sent to England on 30 June 1944 for evaluation at Boscombe Down as the Mustang V and the second XP-51G also went to Britain on 1 February 1945 and was designated Mustang VI, while two more prototypes were ordered in June. These became the XP-51J, first flown on 23 April 1945, with an Allison V-1710-119 with water injection. Both the XP-51F and the XP-51G revealed heavy rudder forces and a lack of directional stability in some flight attitudes and a number of notable modifications had to be made before the P-51H, a refined XP-51F, could become the first lightweight Mustang to enter production. The P-51H differed from the P-51F in having an upgraded Packard V-1650-9 engine fitted with water injection and automatic boost control (the Merlin 100 series was not yet in full production) and driving a four-bladed Aeroproducts propeller. Other new features included a P-51D-type canopy and increased internal fuel capacity. A thousand P-51Hs were ordered on 30 June 1944 from Inglewood with the first P-51H-1-NA flying on 3 February 1945. The P-51H was probably the fastest propeller-driven aircraft actually produced in wartime. Its top speed was 487mph at 25,000ft when used as an interceptor, 450 mph when carrying two 500lb bombs and added fuel. Range with two 110-gallon drop tanks could be extended to 2,400 miles at 241mph or 850 miles when carrying two 1,000lb bombs. Armament was six .50-calibre guns, plus optional external loads comprising the two bombs or ten 5-inch rockets. Ammunition supply included 400 rounds for each inner-wing gun and 270 rounds

A 352nd Fighter Squadron, 353rd Fighter Group, Mustang with a wrecked tail after a collision in combat. (USAF)

for each of the others. Armour included $\frac{7}{16}$-inch behind the pilot's head, $\frac{5}{16}$-inch behind his back, and ¼-inch at the front fire wall.

A few P-51H models reached the Pacific before the end of the war and served operationally. Only 555 P-51Hs had been built when the war's end brought the cancellation of the balance of 2,000 ordered, the last being completed on 9 November 1945, although several more development aircraft appeared. One example went to the RAF in March 1945 and another to the US Navy, which had tested a P-51D on a carrier in November 1944. Also cancelled were 1,700 similar V-1650-11-powered P-51L aircraft and 1,628 P-51M fighters, which were to be the Dallas-built version of the P-51H. Only a single example (the last P-51D-30-NT) was actually completed as the P-51M with a 1,400hp Packard V-1650-9A and flown in August 1945. Forty P-51Ds and ten P-51Ks were Lend-Leased to two Dutch East Indies squadrons but they were too late to enter combat against Japan. China had received P-51C Mustangs to replace the P-40s of the Chinese-American Composite Wing and with the arrivals of P-51Ds in 1945 three Chinese groups were equipped with Mustangs. New Zealand purchased 30 P-51D-25-NTs in 1945 and that same year Australia replaced its P-40s with 84 P-51Ks and 214 P-51D Mustangs from Texas, along with imported components for the first 80 Mustang Mk 20s, which were assembled by Commonwealth Aircraft Corporation. The first was flown on 29 April 1945. With a grand total of 15,386 Mustangs production ended in the USA. They flew 213,800 combat sorties in USAAF service during the Second World War. Licence construction followed for the RAAF with twenty-six Mustang Mk 21 aircraft powered by V-1650-7 engines. Fourteen of them were later converted to Mustang Mk 22 configuration, sixty-seven Mustang Mk 23 aircraft with Merlin 66 or 70 engines and thirteen Mustang Mk 22s for tactical reconnaissance; none of these RAAF aircraft saw service before VJ-Day.

In May 1946 a reserve air unit that was later to become part of the

A 353rd Fighter Group P-51 with wrecked tail on 11 March 1945. (USAF)

A P-51D in the 355th Fighter Squadron, 354th Fighter Group, landing at Ober Olm airfield on 17 April 1945. (USAF)

National Guard was established in the US. From the Air National Guard's formation until December 1948, twenty-eight squadrons of the ANG received more than 700 surplus P-51Ds. These aircraft remained the backbone of the reserve air force until they were gradually replaced or supplemented by P-51Hs. By 1952, sixty-eight of the ninety-eight ANG squadrons were operating both types of Mustang. In July

1947 the Army and Air Force of the United States separated and the USAAF became the USAF. The following year saw the introduction of a new designation system for Air Force aircraft, with P for Pursuit changing to F for Fighter, the Mustang then becoming the F-51. This also affected the photographic reconnaissance versions still in service, with the F-6D and F-6K aircraft becoming the RF-51D and RF-

Little Plug in the 358th Fighter Squadron, 355th Fighter Group, in May 1945. (via D. Crow)

51K. The Mustang remained in US service with Strategic Air Command until 1949 and the ANG phased out its last F-51D in March 1957. In the RAF some remained in use with Fighter Command until 1946, when the last unit to operate the Mustang was 21 Squadron at Nicosia, Cyprus. The P-51K was withdrawn from service in 1951 but the ANG, which operated F-51Ds and RF-51Ds in fifteen wings, did not relinquish their last F-51D to the Air Force Museum until March 1957. War surplus P-51s from both the USA and UK continued to have some years of post-war service with at least fifty-five air forces. The Italian Air Force took delivery of 123 P-51s between April 1948 and November 1950 and a

number of South American countries bought Mustangs in the 1950s. The Royal Canadian Air Force (RCAF) received 130 P-51Ds from the USAF beginning in June 1947. The aircraft was known at the time as the Mustang Tactical Fighter Mk 4. The Philippine Air Force operated Mustangs as their main fighter type from the mid-1950s, the model equipping three fighter squadrons until 1959 when F-86 Sabres started to arrive as their replacement. The Swiss Air Force received the first of 130 P-51Ds in February 1948, many of them ex-Eighth and Ninth Air Force machines. Sweden had become interested in the Mustang after P-51Bs that were out of fuel or damaged had landed there in May 1944. Requests were made to the US Government for a supply to replace their obsolete Italian-made fighters, and in March 1945 the US supplied fifty P-15Ds to Sweden. Wartime internments and more purchases in 1946–48 brought the total of Swedish P-51s (J-26) to 161. In 1952–53 Sweden sold twenty-five to Israel, forty-two to Dominica and twenty-five to Nicaragua. Mustangs once more went to war in October 1956 during Israel's successful Sinai campaign. Many other second-hand Mustangs were sold or given to over a dozen different countries. Filipino P-51Ds attacked guerrillas in 1948.

Although the P-51 had demonstrated exceptional range for a fighter, even greater range capability was required in the Pacific theatre. This had led, in January 1944, to the development of the XP-82 Twin Mustang prototype, the last

P-51D Babs In Arms in the 383rd Fighter Squadron, 364th Fighter Group, 67th Fighter Wing, at Honington on 21 May 1945. (USAF)

propeller-driven fighter purchased by the US Air Force. The P-82 was, essentially, two P-51H fuselages with one port and one starboard wing eliminated, joined together on a single parallel-chord wing section and with a stabilizer and a new tail plane and elevator. The revised main landing gear comprised a retractable main wheel underneath each fuselage and there were twin tail-wheels; the last on Air Force aircraft. Armament consisted of six .50-calibre fixed guns with 400rpg in the wing centre section. Wing racks could carry four drop tanks, up to 6,000lb of bombs or 25 rockets, or a centre pod containing 8 more guns. Power was provided by Packard Merlin V-1650-23/25 engines with 'handed' propellers rotating in opposite directions to avoid excessive torque on take-off. The Twin Mustang climbed far faster than the F-51. Top speed of the F-82G was 461mph at 21,000ft, cruising speed 286mph, initial rate of climb 3,770ft/min, service ceiling 38,900ft and range 2,240 miles.

The XP-82 (NA-120) was first flown on 16 June 1945, a second flew in August and one XP-82A with Allison V-1710-119s was accepted in October. The USAAF placed an order for 500 P-82B fighters but only 20 had been built when the war ended in August 1945, and were delivered by March 1946. Two of the P-82Bs were converted as night-fighters and designated P-82C and -82D, with SCR-720 and APS-4 radar in a pod under the centre section, respectively. The pilot was on the left side and the starboard crewman became the observer/radar operator in each case. The P-82 could be flown from either cockpit, although only the port fuselage contained all the normal flight and engine instruments; the starboard cockpit, for the co-pilot, had sufficient instruments only for relief and emergency operation.

The P-82C was flown on 27 March 1946 and the P-82D was flown two days later. On 27/28 February 1947 a P-82B named *Betty Jo* and crewed by pilot Lieutenant Colonel Robert E. Thacker and Lieutenant John Ard flew 5,051 miles non-stop from Hawaii to La Guardia Field, New York City, at an average speed of 342mph. This was the longest non-stop flight ever made by a propeller-driven fighter. (*Betty Jo* has been preserved in the USAF Museum at Wright-Patterson AFB.) Another P-82 began tests with a camera pod for reconnaissance on 15 November 1948. On 10 October 1946 the USAAF placed a new order for 250 P-82s powered by Allison V-1710-143 and -145 engines, comprising 100 P-82E escort fighters and 150 night-fighters designated as P-82F (100 with APS-4 radar) and P-82G (50 with SCR-720 radar) aircraft. The first of these flew on 17 February 1947 but engine difficulties soon showed that the transition from Merlin engines to Allisons had been a mistake. By the end of the year only four F-82As had been accepted and airframes awaited satisfactory power plants, but from January to July 1948, ninety-six F-82Es were accepted for the only USAF escort-fighter group. As engines and radar became available for all-weather versions, an F-82F flew on 11 March 1948, with APG-28 radar. The USAF accepted ninety-one F-82Fs, forty-five F-82Gs with older SCR-720 radar and finally, fourteen winterised F-82Hs for service in Alaska. Twin Mustang production ended in March 1949. F-82F/Gs replaced Northrop F-61 Black Widows in service with Air Defence Command in 1948–50, while the 27th Fighter-Escort Group of Strategic Air Command used the F-82E as a long-range escort fighter until August 1950. Beginning in September 1948, the all-weather versions went to the 52nd Fighter Group at Mitchel Field to protect the north-eastern states, the 325th Fighter Group at McChord AFB to protect the north-west, and the 347th Fighter Group in Japan. The last USAF squadron to use the type was the 449th Fighter Group, whose P-82Hs operated in Alaska until 1952 when they were retired to be replaced by the F-89 Scorpion.

When the Korean War began on Sunday 25 June 1950, the US Fifth Air Force's defensive capability included two F-82G all-weather fighter units, the 68th Fighter (All-Weather) Squadron at Itazuke and the 339th Fighter (All-Weather) Squadron at Yokota; both of the 8th Fighter-Bomber Wing. The F-82s had their first air combat that same day when five machines from these Squadrons, patrolling over Kimpo

Mustangs of the 531st Squadron, 21st Group, assigned to VII Fighter Command to escort B-29 Superfortresses on their long-range missions to Japan. (USAF)

Air Service Command technicians at Speke near Liverpool in the summer of 1945 working on P-51Ds that are to be shipped back to the USA. In the foreground are 'QL' and 'YC' coded F-6Ds of the 69th Tactical Reconnaissance Group, Ninth Air Force, while 'CY' is a P-51D of the 55th Fighter Group, Eighth Air Force. (USAF)

P-51D *Zoom Zoozie* in the 1st Scouting Force after landing in May 1945 at the captured German airfield at Polzen near Leipzig, which was captured by the 9th Armoured Division, 1st US Army. (*USAF*)

airfield, were attacked by five North Korean Yak-7 fighters. The Twin Mustangs shot three down without loss to themselves. Pilots found the F-82 difficult to land during the day due to the restricted visibility over the nose and the blanking effect of the starboard fuselage. At night the landing lights could not be used due to the blinding glare on the propellers. Taxi lights were therefore employed for night landings, but even so it was almost impossible to make a four-point touchdown since the plane tended to skip on the two main wheels. Twin Mustangs would fly 1,868 sorties in the Korean War, including fighter-patrol, close-support, and night-intrusion missions.

As many as 764 Mustangs were in the Air National Guard and a further 794 in storage. Some 145 F-51Ds were recalled from the ANG and flown to Alameda in California for shipment to Japan on the aircraft carrier USS *Boxer*, together with pilots and ground crews. The F-51D was selected as their main role would be in ground attack, an operation for which they would be more suited than the lighter F-51H. All the Mustangs were equipped with underwing attachment points for bombs or rockets. Within a year the USAF had ten F-51 wings, of which three equipped with F-51Ds served in Korea with the air arms of South Korea (ROKAF), South Africa and Australia, the last named operating some of the 200 Mustangs built in Australia. No. 2 Squadron of the South

P-51 Blitz Buggy *44-63228 in the 354th Fighter Squadron, 355th Fighter Group. (via D. Crow)*

African Air Force (SAAF) flew over 10,000 combat sorties before converting to the F-86 Sabre late in 1952.

Mustangs of 77 Squadron RAAF flew their first mission on 2 July 1950 when they escorted B-29s attacking the North Korean airfield of Yongpu. The next day five Mustangs of 77 Squadron attacked what was believed to be a strong North Korean convoy pushing southwards between Osan and Suwon. Only later was it learned that it was a ROK convoy filled with retreating troops, who suffered severe casualties as a result of the air attack. Meanwhile, included in a US request

for extra aircraft were an additional sixty-four F-51 Mustangs and twenty-one F-82s for long-range ground-attack work. The Mustangs were to be used to form a new fighter-bomber group based on Iwakuni. The Thirteenth Air Force was also ordered to form an F-51 Squadron at Johnson AB with thirty Mustangs taken from storage, and the immediate despatch to Korea of one medium bombardment wing, two Mustang wings and two F-82 all-weather squadrons was requested. There was a critical shortage of spares, which frustrated any move to make good the combat attrition suffered by the Fifth Air Force's F-82s in Korea.

The real turning point in the air-ground offensive came on 15 July when the Mustang-equipped 51st Fighter Squadron

Mr Lucky 44-73041 WR-Z in the 354th Fighter Squadron, 355th Fighter Group, at Augsburg at the end of the Second World War. (via D. Crow)

P-51H 44-64164, the fifth production P-51H-1-NA. (North American)

at Taegu, which absorbed the battle-weary survivors of a composite ROK/American unit, flew its first ground-attack mission. The next day Mustangs of the 40th Fighter Squadron flew to an airstrip near Pohang on the east coast of Korea from Ashiya. This squadron was the first Fifth Air Force unit to exchange its F-80 jets for piston-engined F-51s and the pilots had completed their conversion to the older type in record time. The two Mustang squadrons carried out a series of successful napalm attacks on North Korean Russian-built T-34 tanks, which were extremely vulnerable to these attacks as the flaming jelly was easily sucked into the tank's engine compartment. However, US and ROK forces were driven back towards the Pusan perimeter and the need for close-support aircraft operating from Korean airfields became imperative. On 23 July the *Boxer* arrived at Tokyo and offloaded the 145 Mustangs drawn from ANG units. These aircraft were assembled by the Far East Air Materiel Command in record time and flown to Tachikawa for collection by their pilots, who had been undergoing a conversion course at Johnson AB. The first batch of combat-ready Mustangs was delivered to the 40th and 51st Squadrons in Korea on 30 July, bringing the strength of each unit up to twenty-five aircraft, and preparations were made to move another Mustang unit, the 67th Squadron of the 18th FBG, to Taegu from Ashiya. The plan was to deploy a proportion of these aircraft to the airfields still in South Korean hands at the earliest possible opportunity, but in July 1950 only one airfield, at Taegu (K-2), was suitable for operations even by piston-engined combat aircraft. The third Mustang squadron to arrive in Korea was the 39th, which exchanged its F-80 jets for Mustangs during the first week of August and moved to Pohang on the 7th. On the 11th the 8th Group's 35th and 36th Squadrons also converted to Mustangs, although for the time being both units continued to operate from Japanese bases. By 11 August, six Fifth Air Force fighter-bomber squadrons had converted to Mustangs. When the NKA (North Korean Army) pushed down the coast the 35th Fighter Interceptor Group was forced to fly its Mustangs to Japan. Fifth Air Force Mustang fighter-bombers initially flew strikes from Japan, afterwards landing at Taegu to refuel and re-arm for a new series of strikes. The Mustang pilots operated virtually non-stop for forty-eight hours while daylight lasted, taking an enormous toll on the enemy and by 21 August the Allies had recaptured most of the ground that had been lost during the enemy offensive.

By early October Mustangs of the 39th and 40th Squadrons (35th Fighter Interceptor Group) and 77 Squadron RAAF were based at Taegu airfield. The F-51s of the 18th Fighter-Bomber Group were at K-9, Pusan East airfield, and Mustangs of the 8th FBG began operating from Suwon. However, only half the runway was usable and at the end of the month two squadrons began operation from

Kimpo, where they joined Mustang squadrons in the 51st Fighter Interceptor Group and the 80th Fighter-Bomber Group. Mustangs proved invaluable in the months ahead. In February 1951 the 18th FBG alone destroyed 728 enemy vehicles and damaged 137. The standard truck-hunting armament load for the Mustangs was rockets and 0.50-calibre machine guns. Rockets proved effective against flak positions and soft-skinned vehicles but Mustang casualties

were about 60 per cent of the total loss of 81 aircraft sustained in ground attack operations between April and June 1951. Missions flown by RF-51 Mustangs of the 45th Tactical Reconnaissance Squadron also proved invaluable and the 35th Fighter Interceptor Wing, too, gave excellent service in Korea. This culminated in a four-day period in late April 1951 when its two Mustang squadrons mounted 400 sorties against enemy targets.

XP-82 44-83887, the second twin-Mustang prototype, which flew in August 1945. (North American)

F-82 Betty Jo, which flew from Hawaii to New York in 1947, the longest non-stop flight by a prop-driven fighter. (WPAFB)

Soon there would not be enough Mustangs to go round in Korea and so General Stratemeyer made repeated attempts to replace them with F-84 Thunderjets, but the USAF was reluctant to release more of these for service in Korea in view of the NATO commitment in Europe. A request for F-47 Thunderbolts as replacements for the Mustangs was turned down too. At the end of April 1951, 77 Squadron RAAF returned to Iwakuni to re-equip with Gloster Meteor F8 jet fighters. Late in May 1951 the 35th Fighter Interceptor Wing's 40th Squadron became the first USAF Mustang unit to receive new equipment when it flew to Misawa in Japan for eventual conversion to Lockheed F-94 Starfires. The 39th

Squadron was attached to the 18th FBW for continued service in Korea as the Fifth Air Force centralized its remaining Mustang units. On 20 June 1951 eight Ilyushin Il-10 ground-attack aircraft crossed the Yalu and headed for the island of Sinmi-do, just off the Korean coast, which was being held by a small force of ROK troops. Purely by chance the Ilyushins were sighted by Mustang pilots carrying out an offensive sweep along the road near Sinmi-do. A second flight of Mustangs was called up and they then attacked the Il-10s, destroying two and damaging three more in a matter of minutes. As the Mustangs continued to harry them six Yak-9 fighters arrived on the scene and were promptly engaged by the second Mustang flight. One Yak was shot down. A dozen MiGs that crossed the Yalu were intercepted by two flights of patrolling Sabres, whose pilots damaged four of them, but one broke through the screen and destroyed a Mustang before both sides broke off the action.

It was fitting that the North American F-86 Sabre followed on from the Mustang, which on 23 January 1953 ceased combat in Korea after 62,607 sorties and 194 P-51s lost to enemy action on missions that were primarily for ground support. American fighter designs were largely outclassed by superior Communist aircraft but the better-trained American pilots, many of them veterans of the ETO and Pacific campaigns in the Second World War, triumphed over their largely inexperienced adversaries and usually made up for the disparity in equipment. Several pilots such as Gabreski, Meyer, Mahurin, George A. Davis and William Whisner to name but a few, added to their the Second World War scores with victories in F-86 Sabres in Korea. When the Armistice was signed in July 1953 only one USAF Mustang unit was operational, with the other F-51 squadrons having been replaced by jets at various intervals.

In the 1950s many surplus Mustangs were bought by Trans-Florida Aviation, which later became known as the Cavalier Aircraft Corporation, specializing in conversion to two-seaters for the executive market and also rebuilding and improving airframes for military use. This led to a series of rebuilds and a new Mustang called Enforcer, which in the late 1960s was designed for Counter-Insurgency (COIN) and Forward Air Control (FAC) duties with the USAF. This

F-82G of the 347th Fighter Group with SCR-720 radar pod, in Japan in 1949-50. (Bart Halter)

Rob Davis aloft in his beautifully preserved P51D painted in the markings of Big Beautiful Doll, flown by Lieutenant Colonel John Landers in the 78th Fighter Group. (Author)

version of the P-51, which had an uprated Packard Merlin, strengthened wings and tip tanks and combined a longer range with extra load-carrying capacity, became known as the Mustang II. It was later superseded by a Rolls-Royce Dart version (the engine also used in the Viscount airliner) – the Turbo Mustang 3. Piper Aircraft Corporation acquired the Cavalier programme and in 1971 developed the Enforcer, which led to a USAF contract in 1981 for two turboprop powered PA-48 prototypes, which were built from P-51 parts. These were flown on 9 April and 8 July 1983 respectively. P-51s with various modifications have appeared as civilian racing aircraft. One was powered by a 3,800hp Rolls-Royce Griffon engine, and holds the current world speed record for piston-engine aircraft at 499.048mph. The turboprop ground-attack aircraft was designed to replace the USAF's A-10 Warthog but the military showed little interest and after trials of the two machines produced, both Enforcers were flown to Davis-Monthan AFB for storage.

Among the Mustang's achievements were successes in the Bendix, Thompson and other trophy races and Jacqueline Cochrane set an official 100-kilometre record at a speed of 469.5mph and the three-kilometre record of 412mph. The well-known sporting and film stunt pilot Paul Mantz won the first post-war Bendix air race in a Mustang at an average speed of 435mph. Another Mustang-flying Bendix winner was Joe De Bona, whose extensively modified and cleaned-up P-51C averaged more than 470mph, the highest recorded for a competitive event. This machine was later sold to a farmer who profitably used it in western Nebraska for weather control operations. Silver iodide was burned in a generator located in the aircraft's engine compartment and exhausted inside thunderhead clouds at altitudes of about 30,000ft to induce cloud nucleation and prevent the formation of crop-damaging hail.

Enthusiasm for the Mustang is vast and display examples refurbished by Florida's Cavalier Aircraft in 1967 and even derelict P-51s are acquired to rebuild to flying condition for the air show warbird circuit. All have ensured that the aircraft, which is referred to as the P-51 once more, is actually increasing in numbers on the aircraft registers of the world. There 154 surviving airworthy Mustangs, 53 are being restored and 24 are in store. Today, the Mustang is a living legend and is remembered as probably the finest long-range single-seat piston-engined fighter ever built. Captain Dick

P-51 Mustang in the markings of CY-D Miss Velma in the 55th Fighter Group in formation with B-17G Liberty Belle at Duxford. (Author)

Hewitt in the 82nd Squadron, 78th Fighter Group, at Duxford has written:

Webster describes a Mustang as 'a small, hardy, horse of the western plains.' I'd say it was more like a 'pinto pony with the power of a Clydesdale.' I was often asked which of the two, 'Jug' or Mustang I thought the best was. Each did the job they were designed to do. There were times I wished I had been in the other's seat but I'd never, ever downplay either. Unless you have been there and done both, best to keep a 'zipped lip.' I'll just say: Thank you, Republic Aircraft and North American Aviation. Both were main reasons I lived to tell the tale.

A P-51D in the colours of B7-H Ferocious Frankie *in the 361st Fighter Group, running up at Duxford. (Author)*

P-51 MUSTANG

P-51A, P-51B, P-51C, TP-51B, P-51D, TF-51D, P-51K

P-51D-5-NA MUSTANG
44-13521
(G-MRLL)

In the markings of the 504th Fighter Squadron, 339th Fighter Group.
Captain Bradford Stevens.
*(Flown by 2nd Lieutenant Myer Winkelman when
the original Marinell was shot down over France in 1944).*

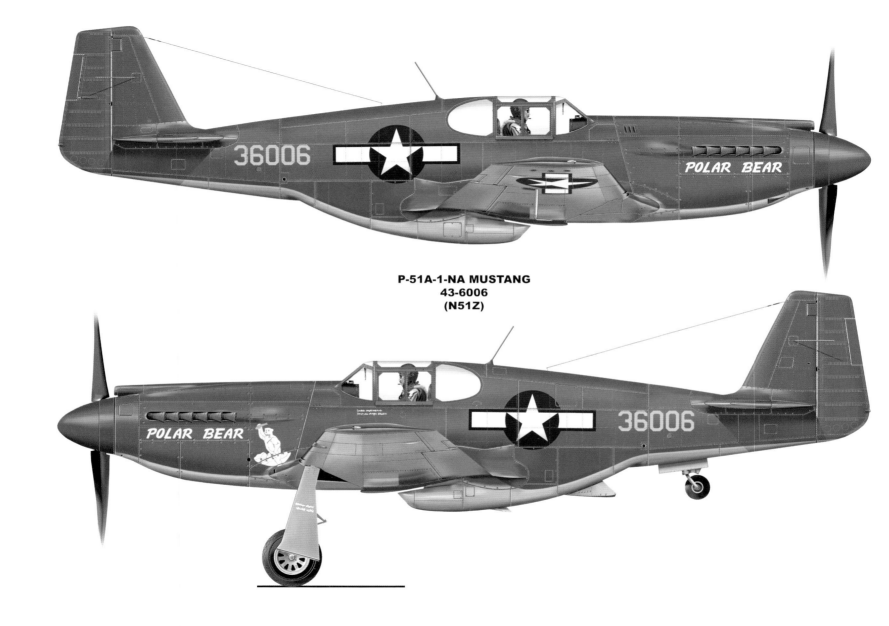

P-51A-1-NA MUSTANG
43-6006
(N51Z)

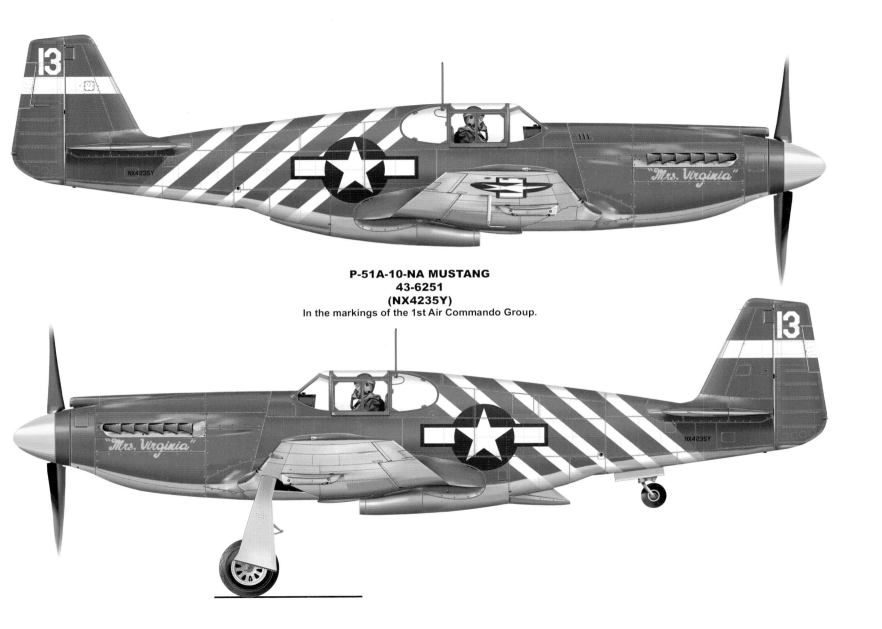

P-51A-10-NA MUSTANG
43-6251
(NX4235Y)
In the markings of the 1st Air Commando Group.

P-51B-15-NA MUSTANG
43-24823
(NL551E)
In the markings of the 357th Fighter Squadron, 363rd Fighter Group.
Colonel Clarence E Anderson.

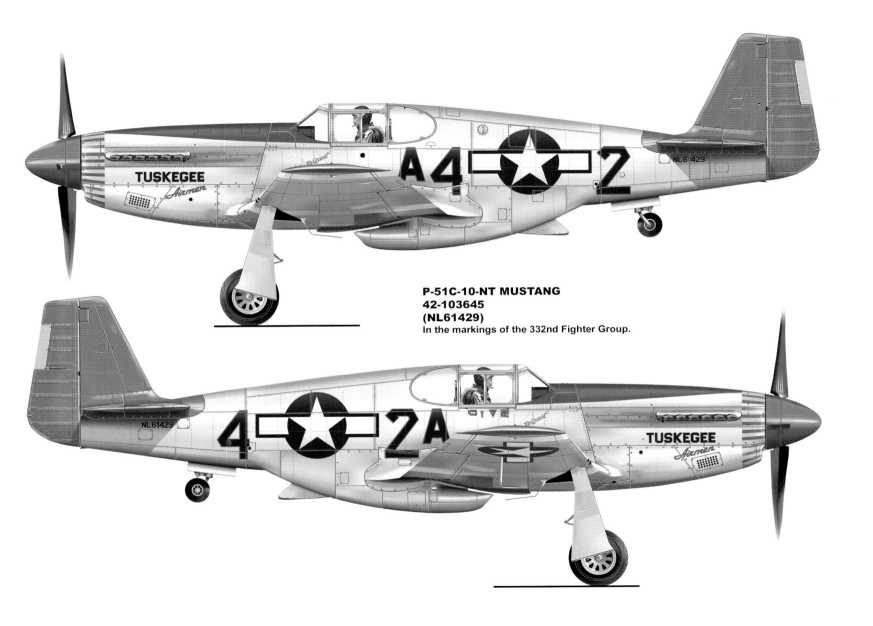

P-51C-10-NT MUSTANG
42-103645
(NL61429)
In the markings of the 332nd Fighter Group.

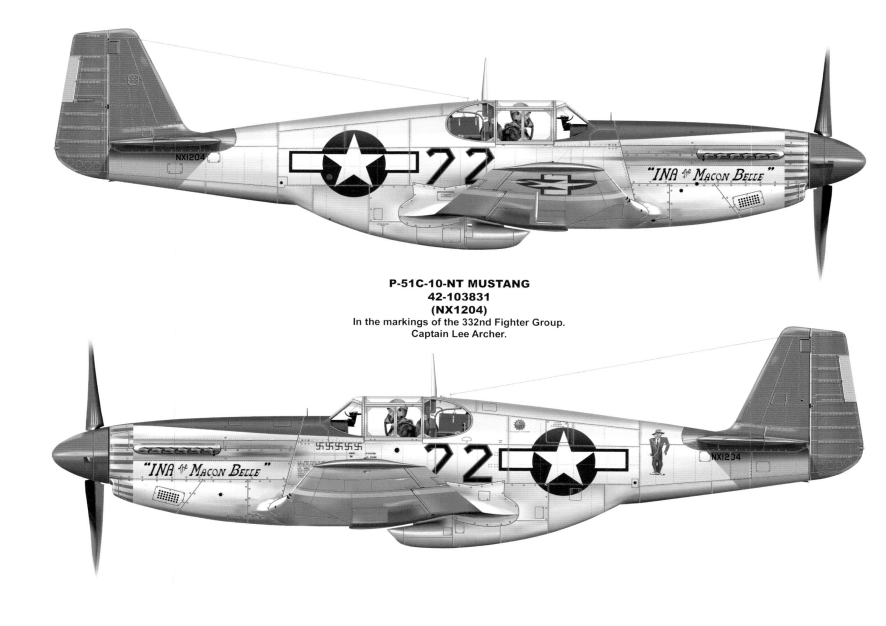

P-51C-10-NT MUSTANG
42-103831
(NX1204)
In the markings of the 332nd Fighter Group.
Captain Lee Archer.

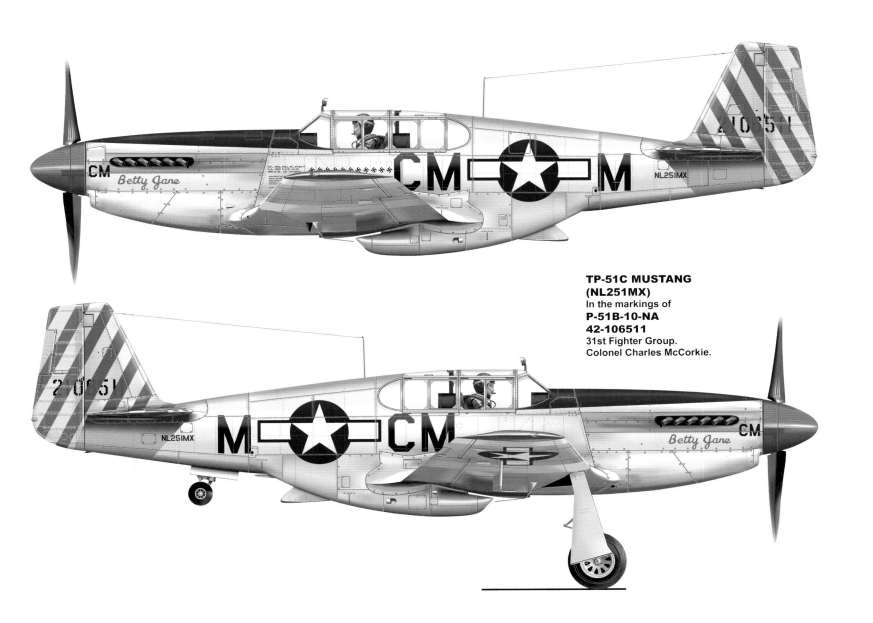

**TP-51C MUSTANG
(NL251MX)**
In the markings of
**P-51B-10-NA
42-106511**
31st Fighter Group.
Colonel Charles McCorkie.

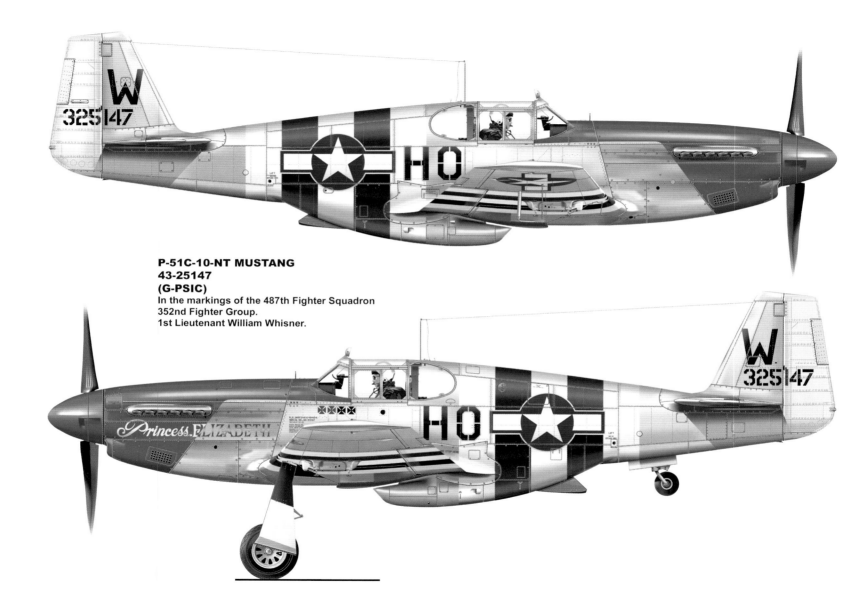

P-51C-10-NT MUSTANG
43-25147
(G-PSIC)
In the markings of the 487th Fighter Squadron
352nd Fighter Group.
1st Lieutenant William Whisner.

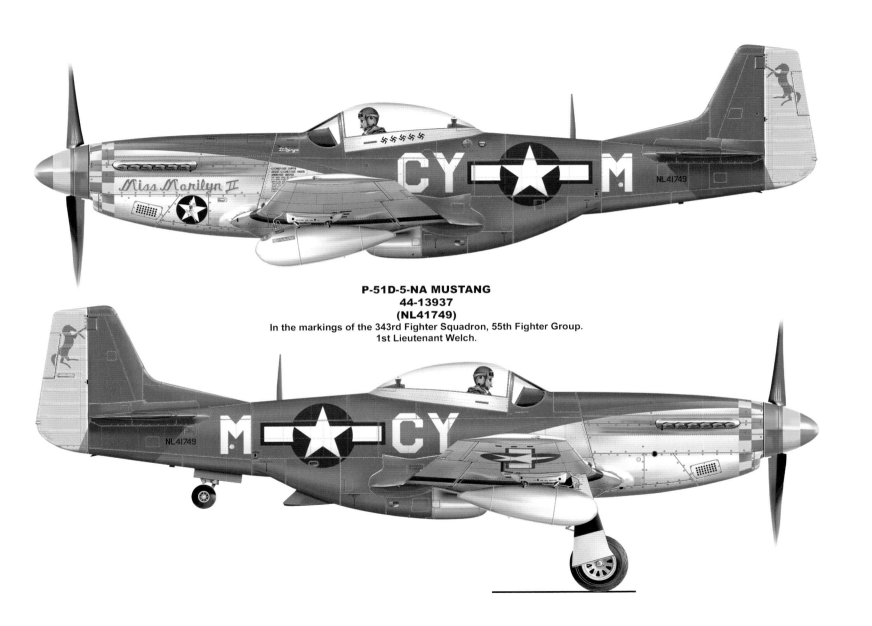

P-51D-5-NA MUSTANG
44-13937
(NL41749)
In the markings of the 343rd Fighter Squadron, 55th Fighter Group.
1st Lieutenant Welch.

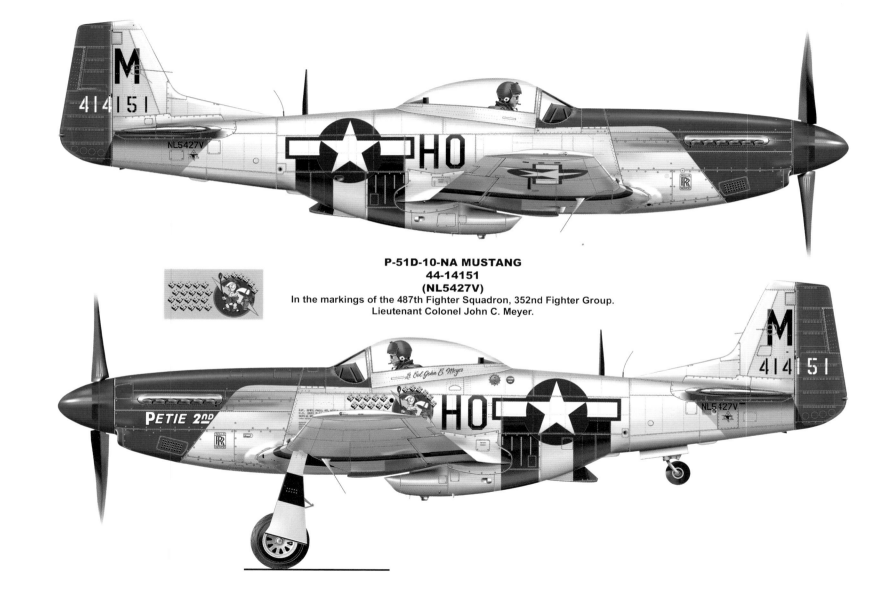

P-51D-10-NA MUSTANG
44-14151
(NL5427V)
In the markings of the 487th Fighter Squadron, 352nd Fighter Group.
Lieutenant Colonel John C. Meyer.

P-51D-20-NA MUSTANG
44-63864
(G-CBNM)
In the markings of the 83rd Fighter Squadron
78th Fighter Group.

P-51D-20-NA MUSTANG
44-72218
(NL351BD)
In the markings of the 84th Fighter Squadron, 78th Fighter Group.
Colonel John Landers.

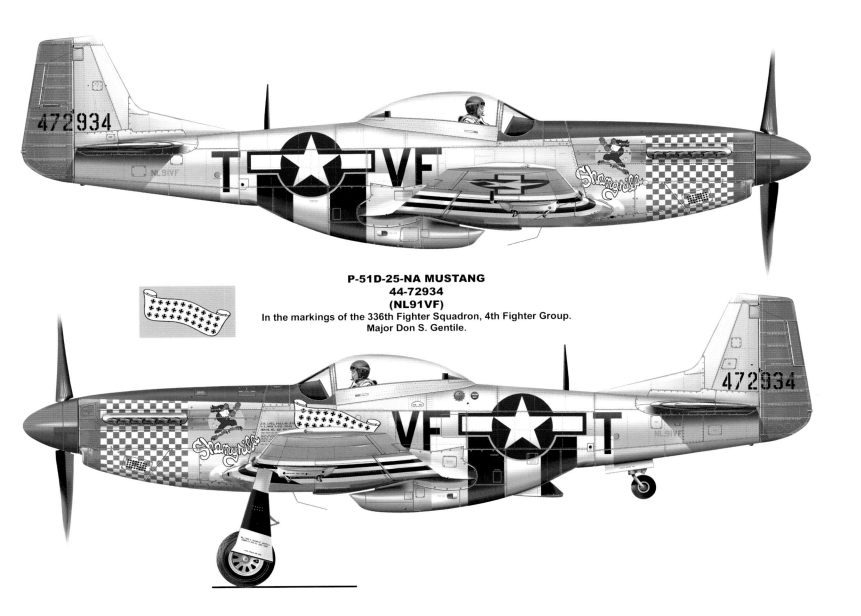

P-51D-25-NA MUSTANG
44-72934
(NL91VF)
In the markings of the 336th Fighter Squadron, 4th Fighter Group.
Major Don S. Gentile.

P-51D-30-NA MUSTANG
44-74425
(PH-PSI)
In the markings of the 356th Fighter Group.

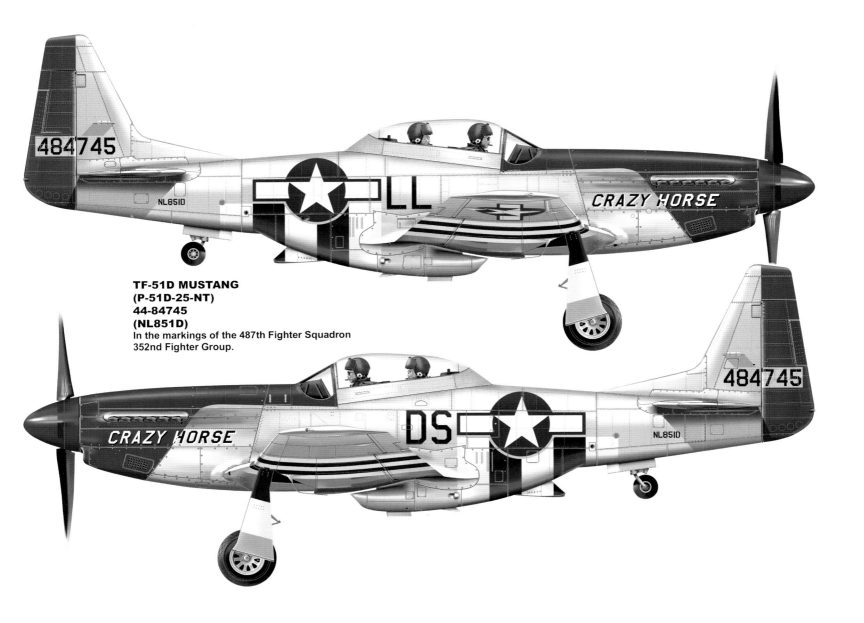

TF-51D MUSTANG
(P-51D-25-NT)
44-84745
(NL851D)
In the markings of the 487th Fighter Squadron
352nd Fighter Group.

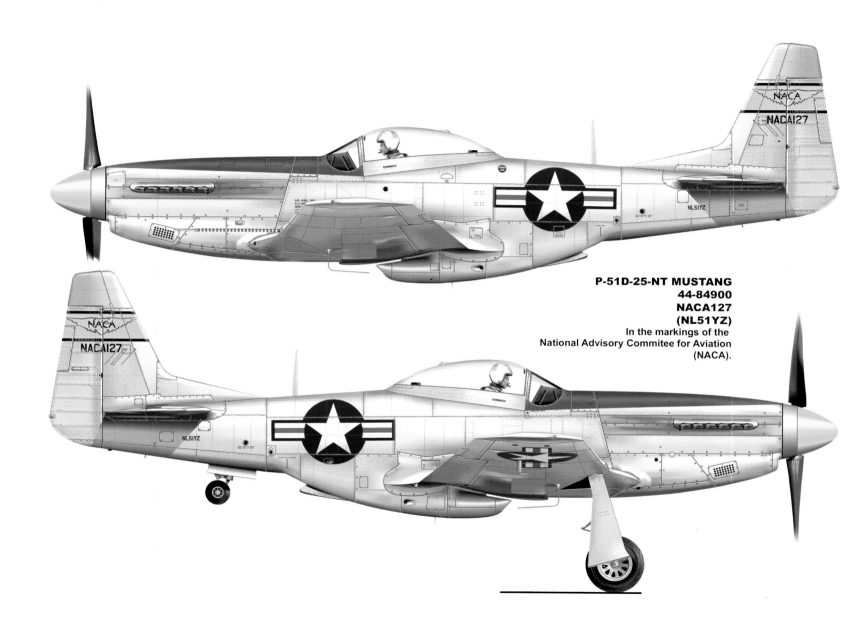

P-51D-25-NT MUSTANG
44-84900
NACA127
(NL51YZ)
In the markings of the
National Advisory Commitee for Aviation
(NACA).

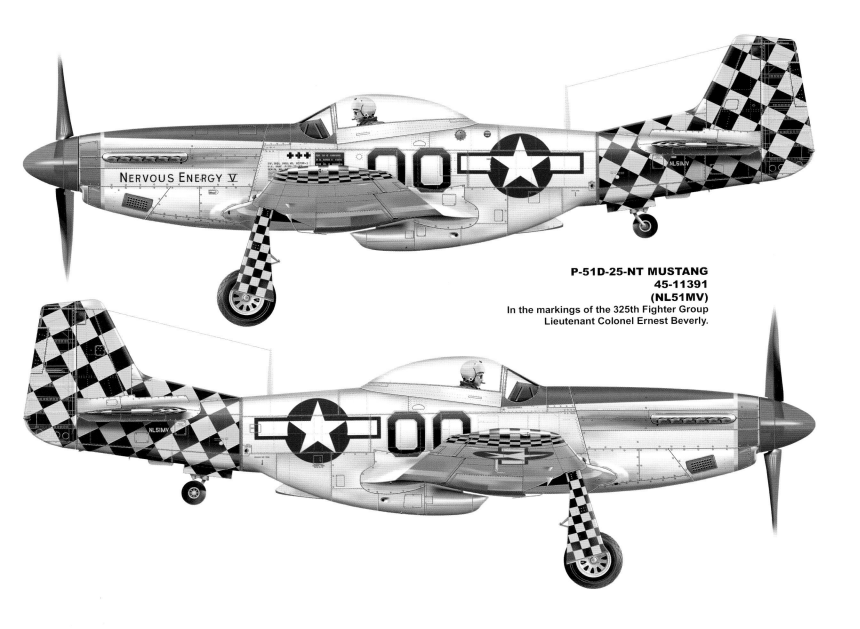

P-51D-25-NT MUSTANG
45-11391
(NL51MV)
In the markings of the 325th Fighter Group
Lieutenant Colonel Ernest Beverly.

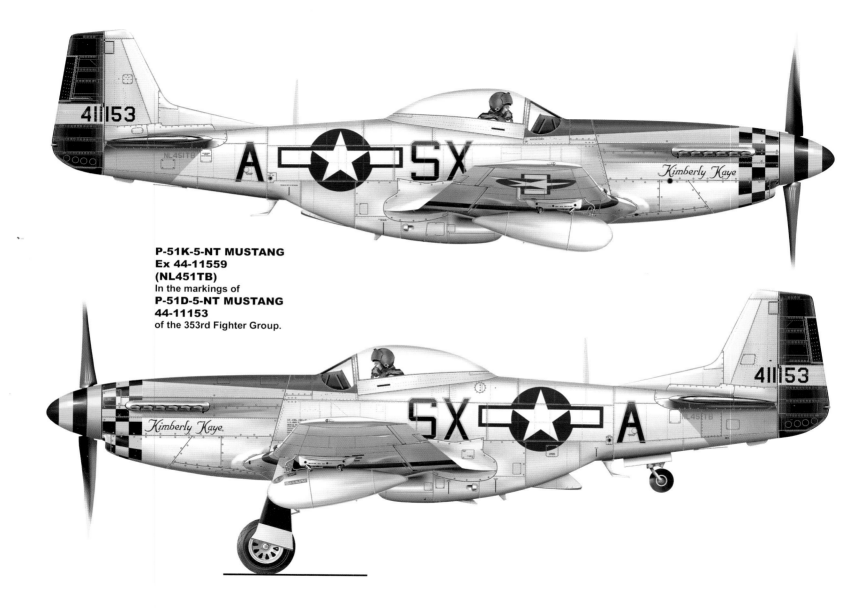

P-51K-5-NT MUSTANG
Ex 44-11559
(NL451TB)
In the markings of
P-51D-5-NT MUSTANG
44-11153
of the 353rd Fighter Group.